12

CW00957454

A Ross Anthology

A Ross Anthology
Quotations Spanning 1,000 Years

compiled by

Jon Hurley

Logaston Press

LOGASTON PRESS
Little Logaston, Logaston,
Woonton, Almeley, Herefordshire HR3 6QH

First published by Logaston Press 1999
Introduction Copyright © Jon Hurley 1999

All rights reserved. No part of this publication
may be reproduced, stored in a retrieval system,
or transmitted, in any form or by any means,
electronic, mechanical, photocopying, recording
or otherwise, without the prior permission,
in writing of the publisher

ISBN 1 873827 95 4

Set in Baskerville and Times by Logaston Press
and printed in Great Britain by
Biddles Ltd., Guildford

Front Cover: The Market Place, Ross, by Cornelius Varley, 1803
(Reproduced courtesy V&A Picture Library)

Contents

ACKNOWLEDGMENTS

These are due to: Heather Hurley; Rosemary Jones; Sue Hubbard and staff at Hereford Record Office; Robin Hill and Carol Robinson at the Reference Section of the Hereford Library; and staff at Ross Library. Special thanks are due to all those recently published authors who have given permission for extracts from their work to be reproduced, and to Ken Hutchinson for the illustration of Defoe's 'woman' and those that 'frame' the text.

INTRODUCTION

The first published reference to Ross, as opposed to the area known as Archenfield, is in the uniquely fascinating Domesday Book. This carefully planned and executed study of what those living in England, rich and poor, owned, was completed in 1086, according to the Saxon Chronicles. This was 20 years after its instigator, Duke William of Normandy, conquered England. The idea, according to the king's grandson, Bishop Henry of Winchester, was that 'every man should know his right and not usurp another's.' In fact it was a massive, all-embracing tax assessment. The king 'wanted to know what he had, and who held it.' Even the name Domesday—the Day of Judgement—was chosen to strike fear into the hearts of potential tax dodgers. Woe betide the seekers of loopholes, because a second army of inspectors were despatched 'to shires they did not know, and in which they themselves were unknown', to check their predecessors' survey and to report evaders to the king. One can only imagine what the reaction would be in these days if a Frenchman were to be so stupid as to attempt to extract a penny tax from the xenophobic British! Evidence was taken on oath, from the sheriff, from all the barons, from the whole hundred, the priests, the reeves, and six villagers from each village. To make it absolutely watertight, as well as rub salt into raw and gaping wounds, four Frenchman and the same number of Englishmen from each hundred were sworn to verify the details.

Nothing much was published about Ross for the next five centuries until intrepid travellers like John Leland arrived, dusty and tired, to take a break from his *Itinerary* to check Wilton Bridge and mention the 'enclosures very full of corne and wood', before disappearing into Wales. The historian and antiquarian William Camden followed with his *Britannia* in 1586, a book which proved to be a landmark in the topographical study of Britain. A Herefordian, Thomas Blount, a lawyer from Orleton, a respected amateur historian, had been collecting material for some time on the towns and villages of his native county. He produced two unpublished manuscripts which, due to his faulty penmanship, and the fact that they lay tucked away in locked drawers and latterly in the Hereford Record Office, have hitherto not been used as much as they ought to be. Celia Fiennes, in 1696 the first lady traveller to record her journey, never reached Ross, probably because the roads were 'deep sand and so stony it made it more difficult to travel.'

It was much later and in more tranquil times that Ross became a honeypot for poets, travellers and artists, who came to gawp at the stunning scenery. In droves they arrived by horse, boat, stagecoach and on foot to sip the local ale, sketch bridge and spire, then damn the scruffy little market town with feint praise. Reams of verse were scribbled, much of it dedicated to Ross' most famous citizen, John Kyrle: landscaper, pipe-smoking bachelor, pub lawyer, and goose-eating, cider-inbibbing friend and confidant to the wronged and the destitute. But why did the man inspire so much bad poetry, some of it penned by our greatest versifiers, including Samuel Taylor Coleridge, who rushed off his ode to the Man of Ross while actually bed and breakfasting in the King's Arms, Kyrle's old house. Over a glass of Malmsey and a wedge of seed cake the esteemed author of 'The Rime of the Ancient Mariner' wrote 'Here dwelt the Man of Ross! O traveller, hear ...' Oh dear.

Ross still attracts adoring chroniclers, among them the inestimable home-grown Fred Druce, author of three books and an entertaining speaker on his beloved town, though he has declined to see any extracts re-published here. A former postman, Fred was well positioned to assemble a fine collection of old snaps and tasty anecdotes about some of Ross' most fascinating characters, many, alas, now gone. Martin Morris, author of *The Book of Ross*, although born in the Forest of Dean, spent a working lifetime as chief reporter for the *Ross Gazette*. For years Martin traipsed around the town in rain or shine, notebook and pencil to hand, writing the every day history of Ross. He must have wisely forgotten more about Ross than any one, for to be a reporter in a small town requires the skin of a rhino and the diplomatic skills of a UN Secretary.

Ross has, in ancient times, always been that modest little town perched on the hill, beckoning to foreigners as they wobbled along the dusty tracks on bockedy mules, or, with staff in hand, waded the Wye at Wilton. The odd poet dropped by to pen a sonnet, among them Edmund Spenser, 1552-99. As secretary to Lord Arthur Grey of Wilton, an adventurer 'who endeavoured to advance his lessened estate by his valour', the future author of 'The Faery Queen' fell into a nice little three thousand acre farm in County Cork in Ireland.

Michael Drayton, 1563-1631, too walked the town in the 1620s. Gazing contemplatively off the Prospect at the glorious Wye below as it slithered around the horseshoe bend, Drayton composed a part of his great 'Seventh Song' — 'Oft windeth in her way, as back she meant to go.' John Aubrey, 1626-97, another antiquary, visited Ross when researching his *Miscellanies*. He remembered 'a long leane, lamentable poor rascal, a wretch who was in the business of sin eating, an old custome at Funeralls.' Daniel Defoe, 1660-1731, whilst touring *The Whole Island of Great Britain*, c.1725, oddly enough reserved most of his perfunctory comments about Ross on 'a monstrous fat woman' he was taken to see by some erstwhile pimp. 'She was more than three yards about the waist' Defoe claimed. In 1732 Alexander Pope, the greatest poet in England, but sadly then an old man who had probably never visited Ross, finally found a subject for a poem he desperately wanted to write about a 'good man'. Every Ross schoolchild has since had good reason to dread being asked in stentorian tones to stand up and read: 'But all our praises why should Lords engross? Rise, honest Muse, and sing the Man of Ross'!

Then, on the 23rd of December 1745, a

Defoe's 'monstrous fat woman, who they would have had me gone to see. ... they told me she was more than three yards about her waist; that when she sat down, she was oblig'd to have a small stool plac'd before her, to rest her belly on, and the like.'

young rector was confirmed at Ross. From that day the town's fame as a tourist resort was assured. For it was thanks to an idea hatched by the man who, according to Charles Heath, bookseller in Monmouth and famed chronicler of the area in the early 19th century, was 'beloved, admired and respected by his parishioners, who considered him not only their Rector, but their friend and benefactor, almost their father.' The man was Dr John Egerton, Rector of Ross and later Bishop of Durham, the well-bred and well-connected 'Father of the Voyage Down the Wye'. Probably tiring of sitting on the sofa writing sermons, Egerton commissioned 'a commodious Pleasure boat' to entertain his friends. The rest, as they almost say, is local history.

Getting wind of this early leisure activity, vulgar tourists, determined to ape their betters, rushed to the riverside at Ross where a boat building industry had been started to cater for this new trade. Soon as many as eight boats, still smelling of linseed oil, were launched and ready for business. Scribblers, of course, continued to converge on the town, some in search of peace, inspiration and gossip, others simply to sneer. William Gilpin wrote a book called *Observations of the River Wye* which appeared in 1783 and was an immediate success, running to five editions. In 1797 Samuel Ireland took a look at the Market Hall, sniffed and said it lacked taste and had nothing about it that was worthy of note except its absurdity, 'which,' he intoned, 'is not to be equalled by the dullest architecture of that or any other period.' The redoubtable Thomas Bonner, an engraver as well as a fine writer, wrote generously in 1798 about Ross in his *Ten Views of Goodrich Castle*. William Cobbett, 1763-1835, Surrey-born radical reformer and subsequent MP for Oldham, galloped his nag down the high street and out over Wilton bridge. His *Rural Rides* says this of Ross—'an old fashioned town, very beautifully situated, and if there is little finery in the appearance of its inhabitants, there is little misery.' Joseph Farrington filled his Diary in 1803 and Robert Bloomfield was welcomed into The Dodgy Poet Society with, 'To Kyrle's high virtues lift no strain, Whose own hand cloth'd this far-farm'd hill.' Thomas Roscoe published his *Wanderings and Excursions* in 1837. Writings by both Charles Heath and the Reverend Fosbroke appeared in several editions over the years.

Lord Alfred Tennyson, 1809-92, also visited Ross, but didn't warrant a line in the *Ross Gazette*. Mind you, that was before Martin Morris' time. Charles Dickens, 1812-70, loved Ross and had a room almost permanently booked at the Royal, (there's a bronze plaque inside the front door recording the author of Bleak House's loyalty). Dickens' agent also lived nearby. This century a quiet nervous little woman called Peggy Whistler moved into Brookend, changed her name to Margiad Evans and vanquished the fey 'greats' with the sharpest and sourest stuff yet penned about the town. Dennis Potter, up there among the best television playwrights and writers, lived in Ross most of his life but as far as I can ascertain never bothered to comment on his adopted town one way or the other. Pity, it would have made very interesting reading. Ross still attracts writers and Peter Terson, author of 'Zigger-Zagger', 'The Fishing Party' and many others, lives in the town.

At one time royals came to Ross and at least two kings stayed in the town, one definitely not by choice! George IV got stuck in the narrow lanes and became so hot and bothered he ordered the streets to be widened, or else! Ross has now largely done with the glitterati popping in taking a look and shooting off. Now it's families fleeing the Black Country for a week's caravanning in Barry, who drop by for a comfort stop and a souvenir pencil, probably made in China. Most don't stay long enough to feel the wind in their ears on the Prospect or walk the path trodden by John Kyrle. Like many another small market town through the kingdom, Ross has changed much during the past hundred years or so when official vandalism began to dismantle and desecrate the old town. Underhill, a great anthill of nooks and crannies, old beams and stone walls, slates and windows, a smelly cobwebbed 17th century pile, was demolished at a time when anything that was thatched, warped, buckled and beautiful was sacrificed in the name of 'progress'. Down went rows of old shops and pubs. Fred Druce says a whole block of history was demolished, ancient windows, doors and lintels were ripped out and sold for £300. When the dust settled Ross was shorn of much of its character.

Unfortunately the destruction didn't end there. Twenty-five years ago a visitor could still stand on the steps of the old Market Hall and look down towards Brookend and see the old benefactor Wallace Hall's house, Springfield, on a hill. One observed cows up to their hocks in buttercups contentedly swishing their tails. Such remaining chocolate box scenes were not destined to last. Can you imagine what might have happened to the wonderful Prospect if Thomas Blake, a shrewd businessman but Ross' most under-rated benefactor, hadn't secretly purchased it around the turn of the century and handed it over to the town forever? Ross was no different from many other small towns, with houses abruptly giving way to fields, many of which would have been visible from the heart of the settlement.

Remarkably, a few old Ross businesses still survive. Ursells, the stonemasons, are still chipping away at headstones. The Crown and Sceptre, featured on the cover of this book, is still in business in the Market Place, and dear old George Nicholls, '74 years in Hardware', is still down at Brookend selling mousetraps, mysterious brooms, brass scuttles and a lot more besides. But Ross is convulsing with change. EC money has helped to narrow the roads, create flowerbeds, put up new metal black and gold signs, finance sculptures of swans and salmon. Traffic is sent thisaway one week, thataway the next. In this rictus of change one wonders what the old benefactors of the past would have thought—men and women who, over the past three centuries, put their hands in their pockets for the town and its poor. Where are the great and the good these selfish times? What would the benefactors of the past have to say about how their little town has changed? Thomas Webb, died 1612; Charles and Thomas Perrocke, 1613; The Reverend William Pye, 1615; Phillip Markey, Gent, 1654; Walter Scott, 1786; Jane Furney, Widow, 1728; John Kyrle, 1724; Eleanor Dubberly, Spinster, 1749; James Baker, 1836; Nathanial Morgan, 1854; James Wallace Richard Hall, 1860; Thomas Blake, 1901; Henry Southall, 1916. In his Preface to the Ross Charities report of 1819 Thomas Jenkins wrote: 'The pious practice of bequeathing to the Poor a memorial of our affection, to continue when we shall cease to be with men, is, as it were, depositing Treasure in our Graves, that will not perish, but rise with accumulated value in the resurrection of the Just.' The old Ross benefactors who never asked what Ross could do for them would have hoarsely chorused 'Amen to that.'

In spite of everything Ross is still there. Wearing a smear of scarlet lipstick, her hair henna'd, on HRT, with both hips replaced, and new plastic teeth. She's swinging, but a little embarrassingly, like a maiden aunt who's been nobbled by the VP Ruby. The Market Hall, where Blake went to school and drew his sums in sand on bits of slate because his parents were poor, is now a 'heritage centre' with locals still selling eggs, honey and secondhand books under its time-ravaged haunches. Some of the quiet inns where poets once gently demurred over which word fitted best into their dreamy stanzas are now smokier and noisier, but surviving with their Sky screens. A few inns still offer tranquil snugs where the fatigued tripper can reflect in a soft chair with his blessed pint. Indian, Italian, Hungarian and Thai menus have added a welcome touch of the exotic to the town's cuisine. The two big hotels still cater for the Hunt Balls and the Rotary 'do's' and the Royal, scene of the Prospect Riots in the mid-19th century, serves lunch to folk who still enjoy the noblest of views in spite of current efforts to spoil it. A night club is a beacon for young hedonists, while the wider community is catered for at the Larrapurz Centre, named after a troupe of local revellers who, way back in the forties, raised the money to build it. There, Yoga, Scottish Dancing, Toddler Mornings, earnest Civic Society speakers and multi-coloured jivers flourish side by side. So Ross, repackaged, with its flower baskets, pedestrianisation, new signs, and mock stone, has, it seems, come to terms with itself. At heart it is still a little country town, not as plain perhaps as when Cobbett came, but travellers who break their journeys will still find a welcome and may be enriched by the experience, even if they don't stay long. For, as far as Ross is concerned, faraway places have somehow always seemed greener.

EARLY DAYS

In the year 918 a large army sailed from Amorica and advanced towards Archenfield, but being met by the inhabitants and neighbourhood, was signally defeated.

Anglo-Saxon Chronicles

Ross was a village in Saxon times and is the reputed site of the death of Edmund Ironside in 1016. At that time the English kingdom was divided between Edmund and Canute, and a slave of Edmund decided to kill his master for the great reward Canute would give him. To that end he placed a sharp stick in the King's latrines (!) and held the candle away as Edmund used them (!!). The King was heavily impaled, as we can well imagine, though it is something I would rather imagine than witness. The dreadful deed reputedly took place at the King's 'Villa' at Minsterworth in Gloucestershire, so why he should have been brought to Ross to die is a mystery. Was he on the way to a holy shrine for a cure? The servant rushed to Canute with news of his great deed. Canute hanged him from the highest oak tree that could be found.

Richard Sale, *The Wye Valley*, 1984

In 1049 some Irish pirates entered the mouth of the Severn, and with the aid of Griffin, King of the Welsh, plundered the country around the Wye.

Anglo-Saxon Chronicles

The famous English archers of history were drawn ... but from the country bordering on the Severn, Wye and Usk. The men of Archenfield were renowned for their valour, and ... when the English marched to war against the Welsh, the men of Archenfield formed by custom the vanguard in the attack and the rearguard in the retreat. There are numerous yews in the district, which provided their arrows, and were used in bowmaking. Long bow strings are said to have been made of plaited silk, and were worth five times their weight in gold.

Anon

1

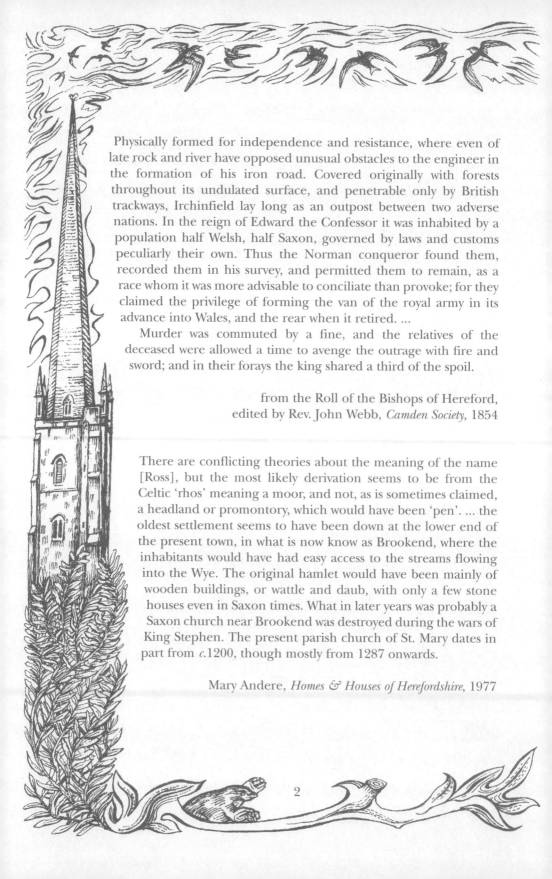

Physically formed for independence and resistance, where even of late rock and river have opposed unusual obstacles to the engineer in the formation of his iron road. Covered originally with forests throughout its undulated surface, and penetrable only by British trackways, Irchinfield lay long as an outpost between two adverse nations. In the reign of Edward the Confessor it was inhabited by a population half Welsh, half Saxon, governed by laws and customs peculiarly their own. Thus the Norman conqueror found them, recorded them in his survey, and permitted them to remain, as a race whom it was more advisable to conciliate than provoke; for they claimed the privilege of forming the van of the royal army in its advance into Wales, and the rear when it retired. ...

Murder was commuted by a fine, and the relatives of the deceased were allowed a time to avenge the outrage with fire and sword; and in their forays the king shared a third of the spoil.

from the Roll of the Bishops of Hereford,
edited by Rev. John Webb, *Camden Society*, 1854

There are conflicting theories about the meaning of the name [Ross], but the most likely derivation seems to be from the Celtic 'rhos' meaning a moor, and not, as is sometimes claimed, a headland or promontory, which would have been 'pen'. ... the oldest settlement seems to have been down at the lower end of the present town, in what is now know as Brookend, where the inhabitants would have had easy access to the streams flowing into the Wye. The original hamlet would have been mainly of wooden buildings, or wattle and daub, with only a few stone houses even in Saxon times. What in later years was probably a Saxon church near Brookend was destroyed during the wars of King Stephen. The present parish church of St. Mary dates in part from *c.*1200, though mostly from 1287 onwards.

Mary Andere, *Homes & Houses of Herefordshire*, 1977

Welsh rhos, 'a moor, heath'. (H.O. [Henry Owen, editor of *The Description of Pembrokeshire* by George Owen] says that in many Welsh, Cornish and Irish place-names, rhos bore the sense of 'peninsula'. The bend of the river at Ross makes quite a definite peninsula, but it is on the side of the river opposite to the town; so the meaning is probably 'moor'.) A variant of rhos is rhosan. In modern Welsh Ross is 'Rhossan ar Wy'.

Rev. A.T. Bannister, *The Place Names of Herefordshire*, 1916

In Ross (on Wye) 7 hides which pay tax. In lordship I plough; another would be possible. 18 villagers, 6 smallholders and a priest with 23 ploughs. 3 slaves; a mill at 6s and 8d; meadow, 16 acres. The woodland is in the King's Enclosure. The villagers pay 18s in dues.

Domesday Report, appx. 1086

At the compilation of Domesday survey there was not a gentleman in the place. The tenure of knight service, however, implies this rank; and Hugh de Walford, who at that time held a knight fee under the bishop, was the first person of rank in the town.

J.A. Stratford, *The Wye Tour*, 1896

A priest is mentioned in Domesday, and it is said that the first church stood in the Brookend, but there are no traces of such a fabric; and it is improbable ...

The town at its first existence began at the Brookend, a low aqueous site, which verifies the etymon from Rhoos. Besides, Domesday mentions a mill, and there is still one on this spot. The surrounding country chiefly consisted of woods, which so late as the 12th century were infested by wolves.

Rev. T. D. Fosbroke, *Wye Tour*, 1838

3

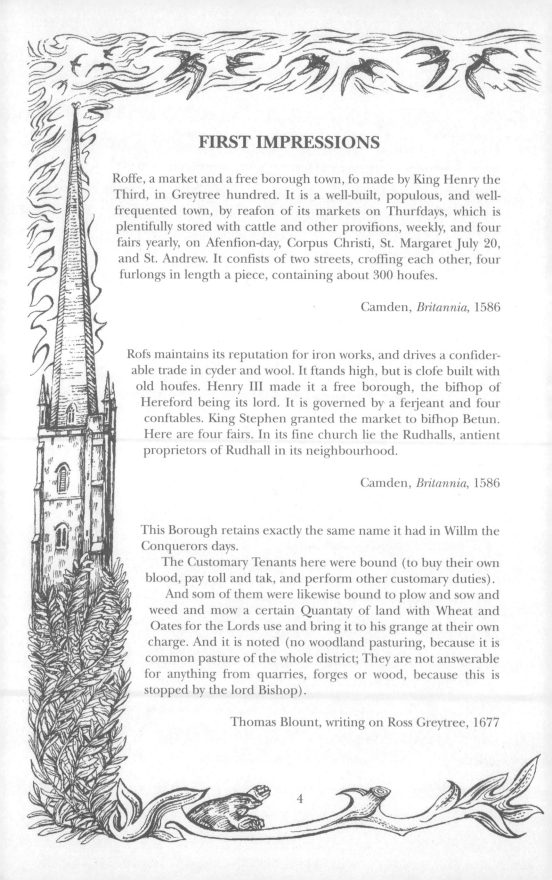

FIRST IMPRESSIONS

Roffe, a market and a free borough town, fo made by King Henry the Third, in Greytree hundred. It is a well-built, populous, and well-frequented town, by reafon of its markets on Thurfdays, which is plentifully stored with cattle and other provifions, weekly, and four fairs yearly, on Afenfion-day, Corpus Christi, St. Margaret July 20, and St. Andrew. It confifts of two streets, croffing each other, four furlongs in length a piece, containing about 300 houfes.

Camden, *Britannia*, 1586

Rofs maintains its reputation for iron works, and drives a confiderable trade in cyder and wool. It ftands high, but is clofe built with old houfes. Henry III made it a free borough, the bifhop of Hereford being its lord. It is governed by a ferjeant and four conftables. King Stephen granted the market to bifhop Betun. Here are four fairs. In its fine church lie the Rudhalls, antient proprietors of Rudhall in its neighbourhood.

Camden, *Britannia*, 1586

This Borough retains exactly the same name it had in Willm the Conquerors days.

The Customary Tenants here were bound (to buy their own blood, pay toll and tak, and perform other customary duties).

And som of them were likewise bound to plow and sow and weed and mow a certain Quantaty of land with Wheat and Oates for the Lords use and bring it to his grange at their own charge. And it is noted (no woodland pasturing, because it is common pasture of the whole district; They are not answerable for anything from quarries, forges or wood, because this is stopped by the lord Bishop).

Thomas Blount, writing on Ross Greytree, 1677

Ross, a good old town, famous for good cyder, and great manufacture of iron ware, and a good trade on the River Wye, and nothing else as I remember, except it was a monstrous fat woman, who they would have had me gone to see. But I had enough of the relation, and so I suppose will the reader, for they told me she was more than three yards about her waist; that when she sat down, she was oblig'd to have a small stool plac'd before her, to rest her belly on, and the like.

Daniel Defoe, *A Tour Through the Whole Island of Great Britain*, *c.*1725

Our road was very good and pleasant, thro Huntley, and thro narrow, wooded lanes by the villages of Lea, and Weston, to the town of Ross in Herefordshire; passing near many picturesque scenes, and to our left nobly wooded hills, belonging to Lords Poulet and Weymouth. Ross, which we rode violently thro, in a shower of rain, is a well placed, but an ill-paved town. We put up at the Swan and Falcon.

Joseph Torrington, *Diaries*, 1787

On the approach to Rofs, a fine amphitheatre of trees called Afhwood fkirts the fouthern bank of the Wye. From this charming fpot, near three miles above Rofs, the annexed view which comprehends the principal objects that compofe the beautiful in picturefque landfcape was fketched. The town is fituated on the declivity of a hill at a happy diftance, and not too obtrufive on the eye; the rifing hills with which it is fcreened give a boldnefs of character to the fituation, nor is the winding of the river, and verdure of the country that enrich its banks, lefs characteriftic of this delightful neighbourhood. ...

The white fpire of Rofs church 'bofomed high in tufted trees' has at this diftance an effect peculiarly pleafing, but on a nearer approach, the town obtrudes too much on the eye, and the picturefque and beautiful, gradually difappear....

Rofs, abftracted from its elevated and delightful fituation, has little to render it worth attention; the profpect from the church yard a fpot to which the traveller is generally conducted on his arrival, difplays a very extenfive and inchanting landfcape both above and below the town.

Samuel Ireland, *Picturesque Views of the River Wye*, 1797

5

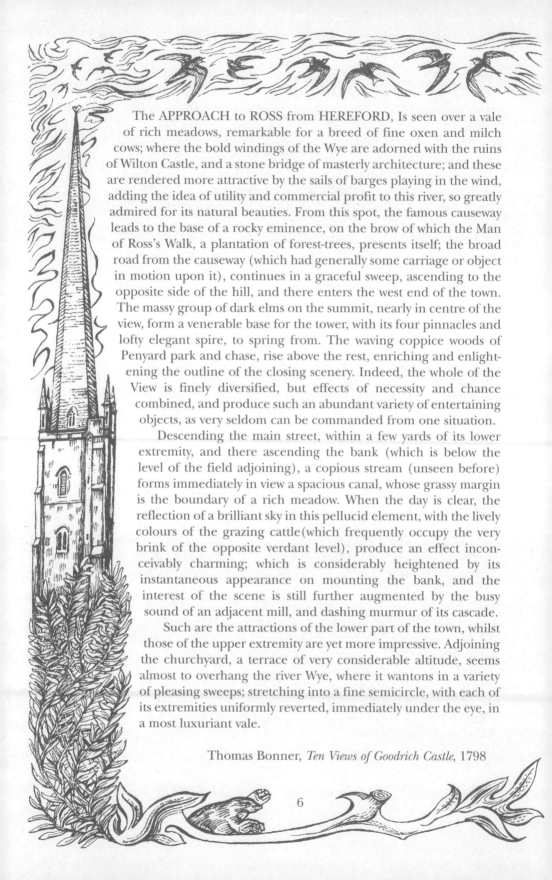

The APPROACH to ROSS from HEREFORD, Is seen over a vale of rich meadows, remarkable for a breed of fine oxen and milch cows; where the bold windings of the Wye are adorned with the ruins of Wilton Castle, and a stone bridge of masterly architecture; and these are rendered more attractive by the sails of barges playing in the wind, adding the idea of utility and commercial profit to this river, so greatly admired for its natural beauties. From this spot, the famous causeway leads to the base of a rocky eminence, on the brow of which the Man of Ross's Walk, a plantation of forest-trees, presents itself; the broad road from the causeway (which had generally some carriage or object in motion upon it), continues in a graceful sweep, ascending to the opposite side of the hill, and there enters the west end of the town. The massy group of dark elms on the summit, nearly in centre of the view, form a venerable base for the tower, with its four pinnacles and lofty elegant spire, to spring from. The waving coppice woods of Penyard park and chase, rise above the rest, enriching and enlightening the outline of the closing scenery. Indeed, the whole of the View is finely diversified, but effects of necessity and chance combined, and produce such an abundant variety of entertaining objects, as very seldom can be commanded from one situation.

Descending the main street, within a few yards of its lower extremity, and there ascending the bank (which is below the level of the field adjoining), a copious stream (unseen before) forms immediately in view a spacious canal, whose grassy margin is the boundary of a rich meadow. When the day is clear, the reflection of a brilliant sky in this pellucid element, with the lively colours of the grazing cattle(which frequently occupy the very brink of the opposite verdant level), produce an effect inconceivably charming; which is considerably heightened by its instantaneous appearance on mounting the bank, and the interest of the scene is still further augmented by the busy sound of an adjacent mill, and dashing murmur of its cascade.

Such are the attractions of the lower part of the town, whilst those of the upper extremity are yet more impressive. Adjoining the churchyard, a terrace of very considerable altitude, seems almost to overhang the river Wye, where it wantons in a variety of pleasing sweeps; stretching into a fine semicircle, with each of its extremities uniformly reverted, immediately under the eye, in a most luxuriant vale.

Thomas Bonner, *Ten Views of Goodrich Castle*, 1798

It is a good, plain country town, or settlement of tradesmen, whose business is that of supplying the wants of the cultivators of the soil. It presents to us nothing of rascality and roguishness of look, which you see on almost every visage in the borough-towns, not excepting the visages of women.

William Cobbett, *Rural Rides*, 1830

I preferred taking the more direct road [from Hereford], which passed through a country of garden-like beauty and cultivation, sprinkled with lovely, cheerful villages and park land, and bounded in the distance by the glorious ranges of blue mountains.

Thomas Roscoe, *Wanderings & Excursions*, 1837

The town being proverbially healthy and pleasant, and, notwithstanding the exposure of some parts, very warm in winter, is a favourite place of residence.

Littlebury's *Directory & Gazetteer of the County of Herefordshire*, 1867

Very few towns can boast of a more lovely situation than Ross, truly called the gate of the Wye, which here bids farewell to the great Herefordshire plain, and enters the broken hills and defiles, through which it flows to the end of its career. It is true that between Hereford and Ross there is some most charming scenery, as a foretaste of that which is to come, but it is not nearly so marked either in outline or character as that which commences so soon below Ross. The town, conspicuous for many miles from its graceful spire, stands at a considerable height above the river plain, towards which the streets straggle down in a rather steep slope, the summit of which is crowned by the church.

G.P. Bevan, *The Wye & Its Neighbourhood*, 1887

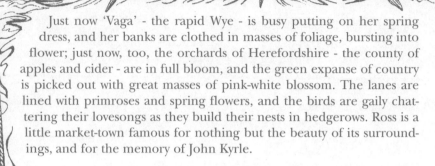

Just now 'Vaga' - the rapid Wye - is busy putting on her spring dress, and her banks are clothed in masses of foliage, bursting into flower; just now, too, the orchards of Herefordshire - the county of apples and cider - are in full bloom, and the green expanse of country is picked out with great masses of pink-white blossom. The lanes are lined with primroses and spring flowers, and the birds are gaily chattering their lovesongs as they build their nests in hedgerows. Ross is a little market-town famous for nothing but the beauty of its surroundings, and for the memory of John Kyrle.

Winifred Leed's unpublished Mss, Hereford Record Office, 1897

The scenery of the Wye was little known to residents in distant counties until Bishop Egerton, during his long incumbency, invited to the rectory his noble relatives and wealthy friends, caused a pleasure-boat to be built to enable his guests to enjoy excursions by water amid scenery which could not fail to delight and surprise that an English river could display such scenes of alternate grandeur and gracefulness, with such an uninterrupted succession of exquisite landscapes. Between Ross and Chepstow, a course of 40 miles, the Wye flows in an uninterrupted stream, and presents through its various reaches a succession of picturesque scenes. At the period of the Bishop's resignation of this benefice, conveyance by water must have become an established recreation, for in 1770, Mr. Gilpin writes: 'At Ross we planned our voyage down the Wye to Monmouth, and procured a covered boat, navigated by three men. Less strength would have carried us down, but the labour is in rowing back.' ...

[The countryside around Ross] in truth is exquisite, for it embraces every glorious inland variety of ground, wood, water and rock. The wood and irregular ground preserve the picturesque beauty from being destroyed by the cultivation. ...

The town itself, sloping on its north side to a brook, consists of narrow streets, and does not resemble country towns in general, the houses being various, and the shops frequently showy. This relief enlivens the streets. The fine, natural situation is, however, spoiled; the town should have been built on a terrace facing the river. The defect is of no moment here, as visitors don't come to see the town, but the country.

Rev. T.D. Fosbroke, *Wye Tour*, 1838

Ross should be visited out of high season to be truly appreciated. Its streets and shops are full of character, and activity centres on the 17th century Market Hall of red sandstone. This pleasant building escaped the 19th century improvers who filled in so many ground-level arcades in various parts of the country, and lively market stalls are still set up here each week.

Rev. C. Read, *Memorials of Old Herefordshire*, 1904

Ross has been called the Gate of the Wye; I confess I never understood why, but it is certain, that for a very large number of people it has a curious attraction. I, too, feel this attraction, and though I cannot explain it, I do not seek to deny it. Yet it is strange that a place with so little natural beauty in comparison with other towns in this valley should have achieved so great a reputation. ...

I have never felt happy about Ross. It stands up beautifully above the Wye, and there are good walks along its banks, and the meadows are green and rich, but the streets of Ross are narrow and possess little individuality.

S. Mais, *Highways and Byways in the Welsh Marches*, 1939

The approach from the river is disappointing, marred by a depressing housing estate and a skeletal electricity station on the left, and the thunder of the traffic on the A40 ahead. But once under the fine new bridge, the town rises above the horse-shoe bend of the river in terraces on which John Kyrle's eigthteenth century town planning is pleasantly mingled with mock-medi-aeval battlements and the imposing facade of the British and Foreign School of *c.*1837. There is a discreet car park, a munic-ipal shrubbery, the inevitable charitable wishing well, and a popular meadow between the river and the town. The whole scene is dominated by the splendid spire of the parish church, rising against the background of Penyard Hill.

Keith Kissack, *The River Wye*, 1978

9

HORSESHOE MEADOW

In the centre of the meadow are still standing the remains of a gigantic oak-tree, which, it is said, once stood on the edge of the stream - and from the very visible addition which has been made to this meadow within the last few years, there is no doubt but such was the case. From some records preserved on the town, it would appear that this tree is upwards of 1,100 years old. A great portion of the remains of this tree was destroyed by fire in 1854.

Edward Cassey, History, Topography & Directory of Herefordshire, 1858

The old oak tree in the centre of the Oak meadow, in 1849 a flour-ishing tree, measuring 29 feet at 3 feet from the ground, is now a ruin, having been burnt in the winter of 1849-50. ...

It appears, from an old survey made by John Green, in 1756, that the old oak was 52 yards further from the bank of the river in 1857 than it was in 1756 - so that it is supposed that in the reign of Henry VIII the tree was a sapling on the bank of the river, and still further back, that it flowed past the whole length of the castle walls, having originally formed one of the defences of the fortress.

On looking the other way, our visitor would miss the row of 13 fine Lombardy poplars on the Old Maid's Walk, adjoining the rectory garden. The vitality of these trees was so sapped by the three cold winters, 1879-81, that after two of their number had been blown down, it was thought safer to remove the rest, and with them a conspicuous object and landmark for miles around.

Henry Southall, Woolhope Transactions, 1883-85

In the Horseshoe Meadow, across the stream, we espy the remnants of a giant oak, estimated to be upwards of 300 years old. A curious circumstance in connection with this venerable tree is the fact that followers of 'the gentle art' may, in the days of good Queen Bess, have sat on its branches and fished in the stream which now, owing to changes in the course of the river, flows at a furlong's distance across the broad meadow..

H. Thornhill Timmins, Nooks & Corners of Herefordshire, 1892

THE CLERGY & CHURCH

It is an historical fact, almost forgotten in the lapse of time and change of institutions, that Bishops in England, during the plenitude of papal power, had places of close confinement for such of the clergy as had been irreclaimably guilty of criminal offences. The church asserted an independent right to try and chastise them; and their punishment, if not mortal, was sometimes pushed to the severest extremity. 'We enact,' such is the rendering of a constitution of Boniface, Archbishop of Canterbury, ... 'that every Bishop have in his episcopate one or two prisons for the confinement of wicked clerks, taken in crime, or convicted according to ecclesiastical censure. And if any clerk shall have been so evil (malitiosus) and incorrigible, and accustomed to the commission of the worst offences, for which even if he were a layman he ought, according to secular laws, to suffer extreme punishment, let such a clerk be sentenced to perpetual imprisonment. ...' One of these prisons existed under the manor-house at Ross. A gaoler was attached to it, who in the time of Cantilupe suffered his prisoners to escape; and the bond that he gave for better behaviour may be cited as the indisputable source from which this information is derived. ...

They were fed scantily upon the coarsest fare, and were denied all access or intercourse of charitable friends; while any hope of being permitted to make purgation was utterly cut off. Their secret subterraneous prison-house at Ross was brought to light when, in September 1837, some workmen were excavating for the erection of a building on the site of the old episcopal manor-house. At the depth of about seven feet they met with a vaulted chamber strongly constructed in the rock. Its walls were five feet nine inches thick; its interior measurement was sixteen feet in length by twelve in width; its entrance was by an aperture in the roof. On each side was a stone bench the whole length of the room, and in a platform on the floor, against the western wall, measuring six feet eight by three feet ten inches, were inserted six huge rings, the purport of which could not be mistaken. They were manifestly intended to receive the chain by which each prisoner was attached to them.

from the Roll of the Household Expenses of Richard Swinfield, edited by Rev. John Webb, *Camden Society*, 1855

The convict Prifon for the Bysfhope of Heriford was at Roffe, now at Hereford.

Roffe at the veri Weft End of the Paroche Churche Yarde of Roffe, now in clene Ruynes.

Leland's Itinerary, 1586

In 1324, [Adam de Orleton] wrote in the Cathedral register: 'When lately I went to Ross to hold a Visitation, a certain son of Belial, William de Irby, Prior of St Guthlac's, canonically ex-communicated, burst into the church with evil intent when I was celebrating Mass on St George's Day and after profane and idle talk, sharpening his tongue like a sword, blasphemously reviled me, though clad in my pontifical vestments and with the clergy and people standing by violently assailed me. Then in spite of my warnings, he stirred up sedition, raised an outcry and assaulted me, disturbing the service and my Visitation to the grave injury of the peaceful King of Kings, in derogation of divine love and in contempt of God's house and to the grave scandal of Christians. I therefore bound him by sentence of greater excommunication. ...

Martin H. Morris, *The Book of Ross-on-Wye*, 1980

[Bishop Richard Swinfield's] retinue on the journey when he entered the town consisted of thirty-six horses, and during four days there was a liberal exercise of episcopal hospitality. The articles of consumption with their cost are enumerated, though not the number or rank of the guests for whom on one of the days thirteen sextaries of wine with ten of beer were provided, and stabling given to lxx. horses. ...

In the reign of Henry VI, it would seem that complaints of the irregularities in inn-keepers, tavern-keepers, and others, had become sufficiently numerous that Bishop Spofford considered it necessary, in A.D.1441, to appoint John Abrahall, steward of his treasury; Uriah Delahay, bailiff of the liberties of the cathedral; Richard Wystaston, receiver-general of the diocese; John Dewsall, John Wellington, and Hugh Carew, commissioners to inquire as to the sale of bread and ale, the use of proper weights and measures, and other regulations in force within the manor of Ross, and to punish all bakers, brewers, tavern-keepers, victuallers, regraters, forestallers, and other offenders who were found acting illegally in their several vocations.

W.H. Cooke, *Continuations of Duncumb's History of Herefordshire*, 1882

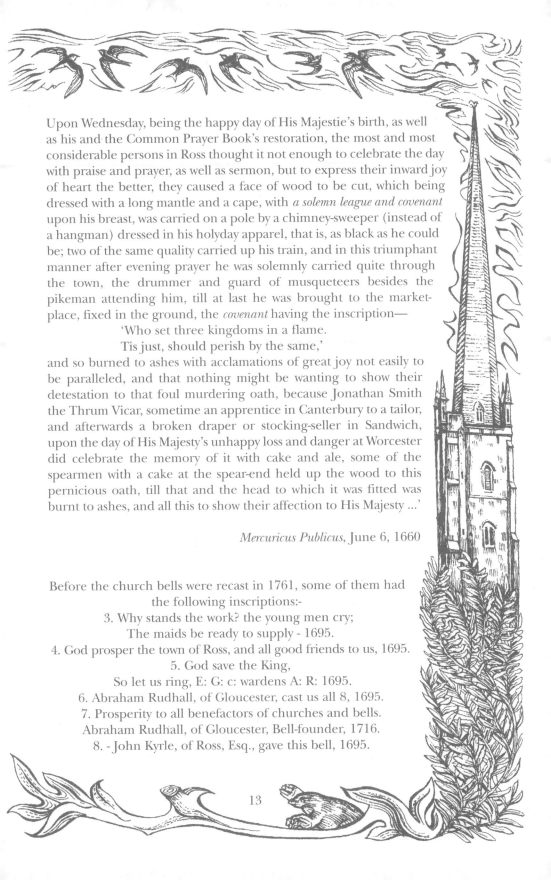

Upon Wednesday, being the happy day of His Majestie's birth, as well as his and the Common Prayer Book's restoration, the most and most considerable persons in Ross thought it not enough to celebrate the day with praise and prayer, as well as sermon, but to express their inward joy of heart the better, they caused a face of wood to be cut, which being dressed with a long mantle and a cape, with *a solemn league and covenant* upon his breast, was carried on a pole by a chimney-sweeper (instead of a hangman) dressed in his holyday apparel, that is, as black as he could be; two of the same quality carried up his train, and in this triumphant manner after evening prayer he was solemnly carried quite through the town, the drummer and guard of musqueteers besides the pikeman attending him, till at last he was brought to the market-place, fixed in the ground, the *covenant* having the inscription—

'Who set three kingdoms in a flame.
Tis just, should perish by the same,'

and so burned to ashes with acclamations of great joy not easily to be paralleled, and that nothing might be wanting to show their detestation to that foul murdering oath, because Jonathan Smith the Thrum Vicar, sometime an apprentice in Canterbury to a tailor, and afterwards a broken draper or stocking-seller in Sandwich, upon the day of His Majesty's unhappy loss and danger at Worcester did celebrate the memory of it with cake and ale, some of the spearmen with a cake at the spear-end held up the wood to this pernicious oath, till that and the head to which it was fitted was burnt to ashes, and all this to show their affection to His Majesty ...'

Mercuricus Publicus, June 6, 1660

Before the church bells were recast in 1761, some of them had the following inscriptions:-

3. Why stands the work? the young men cry;
The maids be ready to supply - 1695.
4. God prosper the town of Ross, and all good friends to us, 1695.
5. God save the King,
So let us ring, E: G: c: wardens A: R: 1695.
6. Abraham Rudhall, of Gloucester, cast us all 8, 1695.
7. Prosperity to all benefactors of churches and bells.
Abraham Rudhall, of Gloucester, Bell-founder, 1716.
8. - John Kyrle, of Ross, Esq., gave this bell, 1695.

PLAGUE

Ross became like a city of the dead or dying. For lack of use, the streets became overgrown with grass, and communal 'plague pits' had to be dug in which to bury the victims. Outsiders from Hereford and Monmouth would not venture near the town, but as the inhabitants of Ross depended on them for food, supplies were placed on Wilton Bridge and the money for it was left in bowls filled with vinegar to act as a disinfectant.

Rev. W. J. Smart, *Where the Wye & Severn Flow*, 1949

'Plague, An. Dom. 1637 Burials 315.a. Libera nos Domine.'
These words commemorate [on the Plague Cross] the number of deaths in Ross that occurred from the ravages of the plague in 1637. In times gone by this cross appears to have been badly used. In 1833, according to an etching from a pencil sketch by a cousin of the late Rev. R.H. Cobbold, the shaft was surmounted by a very poor cross, which unaccountably disappeared. It then bore a square coping stone on which were the words, 'In hoc signo vinces' (the motto of the Emperor Constantine; 'Under this sign thou shalt conquer'). Owing to the clumsy cutting down of a tree, this stone was broken, and also disappeared; but in 1896 the cross was restored, under the auspices of Dr. Strong, and the base, which was partially buried by accumulations of earth, was exposed to view. The orientation of the cross is not quite orthodox, being east-north-east; and the builders of the church adopted the same aspect. But Jerusalem lies full south-east from Ross.

We may add that many people suppose the cross was erected to mark the spot where all who died of the plague lie buried. In fact, there is a common belief that all the victims were interred in a pit over which the cross now stands. This is a ridiculous error. It was originally a preaching cross, probably erected by Bishop Betune some centuries prior to the plague.

The inscription on the base of the cross was cut by the direction of Mr. Thomas Jenkins, a noted antiquary, of Ross.

J.A. Stratford, *The Wye Tour*, 1896

TOWN BUILDINGS

... the Market Hall stands, an ugly monument to the skill of John Abell, dating back to Charles II. It is simply a curiosity. Personally, however, our town would not seem to us to be Ross without it, and we have all come to accept it as an old, enduring, and endearing part of the town.

Alfred Greer, *Ross, the River Wye & the Forest of Dean*, 1947

The Market House, in the centre of the town, erected by Frances, Duchess of Somerset, had, traditionally, John Abel, of provincial celebrity, for its architect, a supposition for which there is no authority; nor does Mr. Blount, to whom he was known, mention the Ross Market House in his list of Abel's performances.

W.H. Cooke, *Continuations of Duncumb's History of Herefordshire*, 1882

The heavy mafs of building called the Town Hall, from its general appearance conveys a faint idea of the worft ftyle of Saxon architecture, it is a ponderous and unmeaning heap of ftone, huddled together in the taftelefs reign of James the firft, by one John Abel who erected a fimilar building at Hereford; they vie with each other in want of tafte, and have nothing to render them worthy notice but their abfurdity, which I believe is not be be equalled by the dulleft architect of that or any other period.

Samuel Ireland, *Picturesque Views of the River Wye*, 1797

The most striking object in the town is the market-house, built about the year 1670 by its inhabitants, which stands well to the view of returning from the lower extremity, already described. The mouldering quality of the stone is unfavourable to its long duration, but the arrangement and form of the building are by no means unworthy of notice. Ascending to it by several steps,

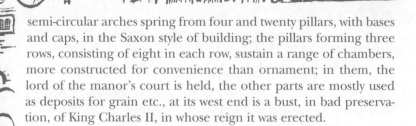

semi-circular arches spring from four and twenty pillars, with bases and caps, in the Saxon style of building; the pillars forming three rows, consisting of eight in each row, sustain a range of chambers, more constructed for convenience than ornament; in them, the lord of the manor's court is held, the other parts are mostly used as deposits for grain etc., at its west end is a bust, in bad preservation, of King Charles II, in whose reign it was erected.

Thomas Bonner, *Ten Views of Goodrich Castle*, 1798

... 50 years ago, the west-end corner of the [Market] hall was perhaps the most attractive portion of the building, at any rate to the lads and lasses of that day. In this corner was situated a rude shop ... which was kept by a notability named Mary Davies, who lodged in Dean Hill, near the old Trumpet public house. 'Mary' was a purveyor of sweets, black humbugs, fruit, and notably fruit tarts, which it is needless to say was hardly of the flavour and finish of confectionery of the present day. The pastry was baked, or rather toasted, on a trippet in front of the fire, and as the frolicsome and tasty boys and girls went to spend their surplus coppers they were required to hold the tart gently in one hand, take off the tip, and wait while Mary placed three gooseberries in the crust, and then brought into requisition a well known and popular earthenware tea pot, which after long and faithful service could only boast of half a spout, from which was poured a quantity of treacle and water to give the fruit a luscious flavour. The fireplace was at the end of the south side of the hall, and the chimney was carried up on the outside of the building, presenting a very ugly appearance, repugnant to the admirers of the Italian architecture. This has been removed, and the part where the flue hitherto existed has been filled with red sandstone, so as to present a uniform appearance with the remainder of the building. While the men engaged in the erection of a lamp in the Market Place, opposite the west end of the hall, were digging out a deep hole in the centre of the street, they discovered a very substantial foundation, the origin of which is at present a mystery. It appeared to be composed of black brick, and stone which resembled that which was used in building the spire of Ross Parish Church. The mortar was thought to be mixed in Aberthaw lime. Some who saw it were of the opinion that the foundation appeared to have been burnt, and at a

very remote date, and, thus massed together, it had the appearance of an ancient British forge used long before the Market House was built, but we are unable to ascertain any reliable particulars beyond the fact it was composed of brick and stone.

J.A. Stratford, *The Wye Tour*, 1896

The town consists of narrow streets, and does not look like country-towns in general, two continuous lines of ale-houses, in a wide road, but like the trading streets of a city, especially of Bristol, the houses being various, and the shops frequently showy. This relief enlivens the narrow streets, and removes the remark of the caricaturist Woodward, that the dullness of country towns is such, that one would think the inhabitants were all asleep at noon-day. The fine natural situation is however spoiled. The town should have been built on a terrace upon the brow of the river. But the defect here is of no moment, as visitors do not come to Ross on account of the town, but of the country.

Rev. T.D. Fosbroke, *The Wye Tour*, 1826

The streets are in general wide, and have, within the last few years, been greatly improved; common sewers having been laid down, which carry off the filth. A nightly watch has also been lately established. The houses were formerly built of wood, and there are some few still remaining; but of late years many brick buildings have been erected, which make a better and more regular appearance. The number of houses in 1821 was five hundred and eighty-five; inhabitants, two thousand, nine hundred and fifty-seven.

T.B. Watkins, *The Ross Guide*, 1827

The town consists chiefly of two streets, crossing each other, which are narrow and badly paved; and the houses generally are old and ill-constructed.

Samuel Lewis, *A Topographical Dictionary of England*, 1845

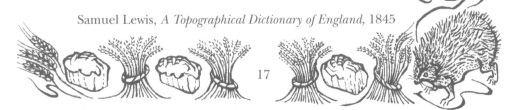

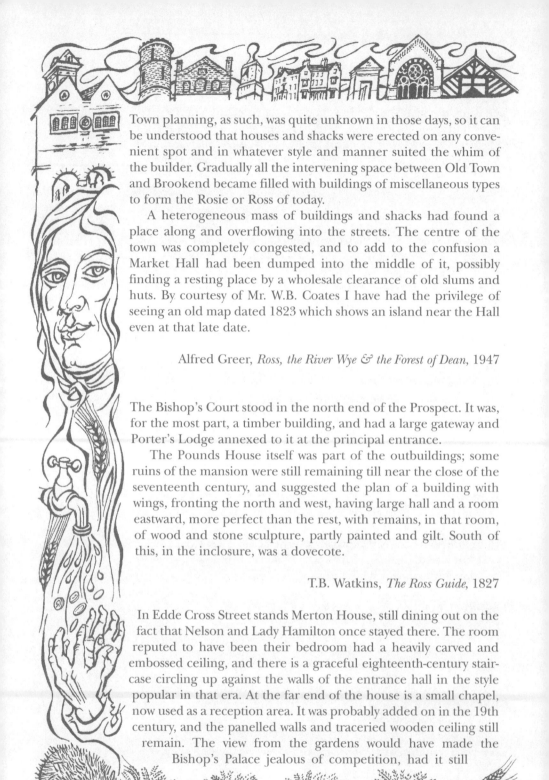

Town planning, as such, was quite unknown in those days, so it can be understood that houses and shacks were erected on any convenient spot and in whatever style and manner suited the whim of the builder. Gradually all the intervening space between Old Town and Brookend became filled with buildings of miscellaneous types to form the Rosie or Ross of today.

A heterogeneous mass of buildings and shacks had found a place along and overflowing into the streets. The centre of the town was completely congested, and to add to the confusion a Market Hall had been dumped into the middle of it, possibly finding a resting place by a wholesale clearance of old slums and huts. By courtesy of Mr. W.B. Coates I have had the privilege of seeing an old map dated 1823 which shows an island near the Hall even at that late date.

Alfred Greer, *Ross, the River Wye & the Forest of Dean*, 1947

The Bishop's Court stood in the north end of the Prospect. It was, for the most part, a timber building, and had a large gateway and Porter's Lodge annexed to it at the principal entrance.

The Pounds House itself was part of the outbuildings; some ruins of the mansion were still remaining till near the close of the seventeenth century, and suggested the plan of a building with wings, fronting the north and west, having large hall and a room eastward, more perfect than the rest, with remains, in that room, of wood and stone sculpture, partly painted and gilt. South of this, in the inclosure, was a dovecote.

T.B. Watkins, *The Ross Guide*, 1827

In Edde Cross Street stands Merton House, still dining out on the fact that Nelson and Lady Hamilton once stayed there. The room reputed to have been their bedroom had a heavily carved and embossed ceiling, and there is a graceful eighteenth-century staircase circling up against the walls of the entrance hall in the style popular in that era. At the far end of the house is a small chapel, now used as a reception area. It was probably added on in the 19th century, and the panelled walls and traceried wooden ceiling still remain. The view from the gardens would have made the Bishop's Palace jealous of competition, had it still

been in existence, for Merton House overlooks the lovely sweep of the Wye and the far line of hills to the west and east. ...

The domestic architecture is a delight with a profusion of variety in stone, wood and 'black and white'. There are Georgian houses in the classical style with tall pilasters and Doric porches, a house with Gothic windows and battlements, imitation Tudor with bargeboards, a Dutch gable, a mock ruin, a polygonal tower in a garden, the prison reconstructed as a house.

Mary Andere, *Homes & Houses of Herefordshire*, 1977

Visitors may be interested to learn that excavation in most of the gardens in Broad Street would reveal not only the sites of very early houses, but often complete rooms with their stone walls still standing in good condition, testifying to the skilled craftsmanship of those ancient masons. Most of today's shops have undergone extensive frontal modifications from time to time, but examination of the layout of their interiors would show these reforms to be only skin deep. In fact the alterations can almost date themselves to the thoughtful person.

Alfred Greer, *Ross, the River Wye & the Royal Forest of Dean*, 1947

The Corn Exchange, erected in 1862, is situated in High Street, and has a very noble and imposing appearance; the principal facade is executed in Boxhill stone, Italian design with a Doric order surmounted by an Ionic. Thomas Nicholson, Esq., of Hereford, was the architect, and the building was erected at a cost of about £4,000. The Hall, a very capacious and noble room, is used for lectures, concerts, public meetings, &c. There is also a Subscription Reading Room, handsomely furnished, for the gentlemen and tradesmen of the town, and a Reading Room and Public Library, for mechanics and others.

The Royal Hotel (erected in 1837) adjoins the Prospect, and commands the charming scenery for which that eminence is so justly celebrated. The salubrity of the site is undeniable. ...

Littlebury's *Directory & Gazetteer of the County of Herefordshire*, 1867

JOHN KYRLE

Mr. Kyrle was full 5 feet 10 inches, if not 6 feet high, strong and lusty made, jolly and ruddy in the face, with a large nose. Respecting the plainness of his dress, which was a dark brown suit, all the same colour, Mrs. Clarke, of the Hill, admits 'he was quite a plain country gentleman.'

Charles Heath, *Excursion Down the Wye*, 1828

1733. April. The man of Ross, whose name was Kyrle, was never married. He was a very humble, good-natured man. He was a man of little or no literature. He would tell people when they dined or supped with him, that he would, if they pleased, let them have wine, but that his own drink was cider, and that he found it most agreeable. He smoked tobacco, and would generally smoke two pipes either at home or elsewhere.

1734. April. Mr. Matthew Gibson, Rector of Abbey Dore, called on me. He said he knew Mr. Kirle very well, and that his wife was his near relation, I think her uncle. He said that Mr. Kirle did a great deal of good, but that 'twas all out of vanity and ostentation, being the vainest man living, and that he always hated his relations and would never look upon nor do anything for them, tho' many were very poor.

Thomas Hearne, 1678-1735, *Remarks & Collections*

His hobby, namely; Horticulture and Planting, was truly Silurian; and in all respects, he was a genuine Herefordshire Man. In addition to his glass bottle and spade, may be mentioned his watering pot, which he frequently carried, and with his own hands watered the trees he had newly set.

Rev. T.D. Fosbroke, *Wye Tour*, 1826

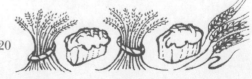

Mr. Kyrle was a man that took little or no delight in what the world calls company. All his pleasure seemed centred in executing or promoting some present good or future advantage. Buying and planting young trees, laying out walks, and such parts of ornamental gardening, were the employments of his later years ... And when his own estate did not claim his attention, he would ask permission to render service, of a like kind, to his neighbours. With a spade on his shoulder, and a glass-bottle of liquor in his hand, he used to walk from his house (late the King's Arms), to his fields, and back again, several times every day, and was always assisted by two or three, sometimes more, workmen.

Charles Heath, *Excursion Down the Wye*, 1828

He worked like a yeoman on the land, and, - here was his strength - had little literary culture. He drank cider and ale and liked good English joints. He smoked a pipe, and never married - his one fault.

Edward Hutton, *A Book of the Wye*, 1911

A theatrical company having obtained permiffion to perform in Rofs, Mr. Kyrle was induced to attend an evening's reprefentation. When the hour arrived, he went to the Houfe, handfomely dreffed, and afked the door-keeper what was the price of admiffion? who, judging by the appearance of Mr. Kyrle, that he was a perfon of fortune, informed him 'half a crown'. 'Ods bud, ods bud', replied Mr. Kyrle, 'that is too much,' and went away home. He then changed his drefs, and, putting on the cloaths he ufually wore in the fields, repaired a fecond time to the theatre, when, on afking the fame queftion, he was anfwered, 'only sixpence for a farmer'; this he immediately paid, and went in. As foon as he entered, the audience, who knew him, rofe from their feats, and made room for Mr. Kyrle to take the place he beft chofe - but inftead of accepting the accommodation, he remained at the back part of the theatre, defiring the company to be feated, for he never got two shillings so soon in his life.

Charles Heath, *Excursion Down the Wye from Ross to Monmouth,*
1799

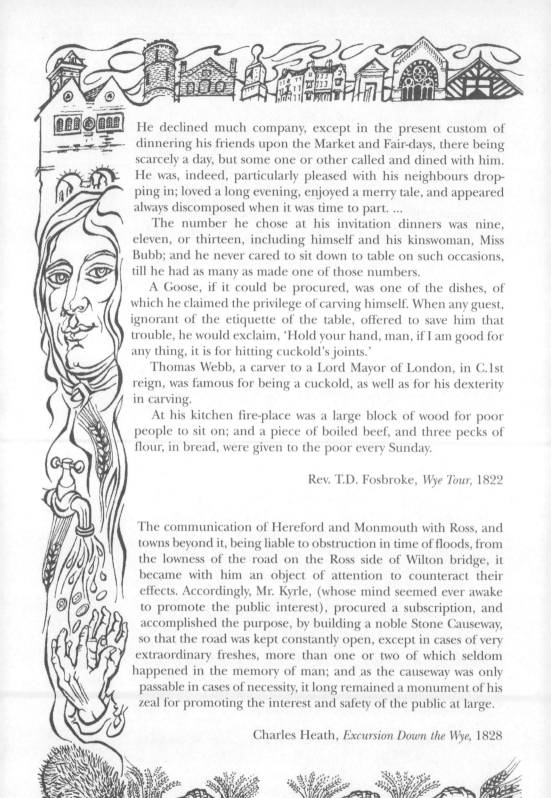

He declined much company, except in the present custom of dinnering his friends upon the Market and Fair-days, there being scarcely a day, but some one or other called and dined with him. He was, indeed, particularly pleased with his neighbours dropping in; loved a long evening, enjoyed a merry tale, and appeared always discomposed when it was time to part. ...

The number he chose at his invitation dinners was nine, eleven, or thirteen, including himself and his kinswoman, Miss Bubb; and he never cared to sit down to table on such occasions, till he had as many as made one of those numbers.

A Goose, if it could be procured, was one of the dishes, of which he claimed the privilege of carving himself. When any guest, ignorant of the etiquette of the table, offered to save him that trouble, he would exclaim, 'Hold your hand, man, if I am good for any thing, it is for hitting cuckold's joints.'

Thomas Webb, a carver to a Lord Mayor of London, in C.1st reign, was famous for being a cuckold, as well as for his dexterity in carving.

At his kitchen fire-place was a large block of wood for poor people to sit on; and a piece of boiled beef, and three pecks of flour, in bread, were given to the poor every Sunday.

Rev. T.D. Fosbroke, *Wye Tour*, 1822

The communication of Hereford and Monmouth with Ross, and towns beyond it, being liable to obstruction in time of floods, from the lowness of the road on the Ross side of Wilton bridge, it became with him an object of attention to counteract their effects. Accordingly, Mr. Kyrle, (whose mind seemed ever awake to promote the public interest), procured a subscription, and accomplished the purpose, by building a noble Stone Causeway, so that the road was kept constantly open, except in cases of very extraordinary freshes, more than one or two of which seldom happened in the memory of man; and as the causeway was only passable in cases of necessity, it long remained a monument of his zeal for promoting the interest and safety of the public at large.

Charles Heath, *Excursion Down the Wye*, 1828

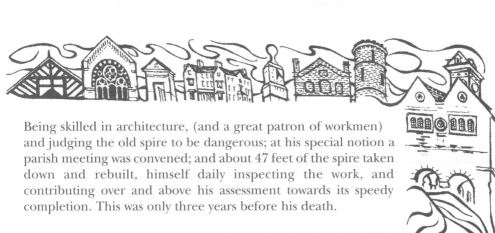

Being skilled in architecture, (and a great patron of workmen) and judging the old spire to be dangerous; at his special notion a parish meeting was convened; and about 47 feet of the spire taken down and rebuilt, himself daily inspecting the work, and contributing over and above his assessment towards its speedy completion. This was only three years before his death.

Rev. T.D. Fosbroke, *Wye Tour*, 1833

Mr. Kyrle had a closet well stored with drugs, and he and his house-keeper, Miss Judith Bubb, under his directions, prepared and gave medicine to all the sick poor, who applied to them, and frequently sent them broth and other nourishment. Miss Bubb was his kinswoman, and both made a practice of attending the funerals of the poor, and generally had some concern in the management; going to the house, and accompanying them to the grave.

Rev. T.D. Fosbroke, *Wye Tour*, 1838

At the chiming of the bell, all business ceased with him - he washed his hands and retired.

Kate Riley, *Tales of Old Ross*, 1921

When he died, at the great age of eighty-seven, Kyrle was said to have been penniless, having literally run out of money on the day of his death. If this is true, it is quite extraordinary and confirms the author's opinion that parents should leave their children only that which is vital to their (the parents) continued life - house, some money, etc., - and a bill for the funeral.

Kyrle's benefactions were impressive, but unlikely to have achieved any great and lasting fame - indeed within a few years of his death he was largely forgotten.

Anon

Mr. Kyrle lay ill for about a fortnight before he died, but not with any particular visitation of Providence, - it was a gradual decay of Nature.

Soon after his death was made public, the BODY LAY IN STATE at his own house, for NINE DAYS. ... The room appropriated for its reception was the parlour, on the right hand side of what was the kitchen; which was hung with black cloth, covered with a black velvet pall, and at each end of the coffin was placed a mute; but no person was permitted to approach very near, - or to lift up the pall, to see in what wood or substance the body was inclosed. People came from all parts, both far and near, to view him lie in state, - never having heard of or seen such a ceremony before in their lives. ... Public respect continued its attention to the very last moment, - the church as well as the chancel being filled with spectators. ...

On inquiry, if the inhabitants expressed their esteem, by going into mourning, [it was] observed, 'That the town did not manifest its regret, by any external mark, or change of dress, but lamented in a general strain of sorrow, that it would never again see so good a man!'

Charles Heath, *Excursion Down the Wye from Ross to Monmouth*, 1799

The place of Mr. Kyrle's interment was, by his express desire, at the feet of his dear friend Dr. Whiting; but there certainly was not an inscription stone over his vault, until Mr. Walter Kyrle placed the flat stone there about the year 1750; but on the wall adjoining, were the initials J.K. neatly done by Thomas Hardwick, parish clerk, and master of the Blue Coat School. There is a bust in relief of the Man of Ross on his monument, executed from a likeness taken when he was about 60, but there is no authenticated portrait of him now at any inn, or public place in the town.

J.A. Stratford, *The Wye Tour*, 1896

He was borne to the grave by his workmen with usual atten-
dants, and male and female mourners, and amidst the whole population of the parish of Ross. This affecting solemnity took place on
the evening of November 20, 1724. When the Church was newly
pewed, about twenty years after his death, the rector and parishioners previously resolved that Mr. Kyrle's pew should remain, as it
does to the present day, in its original situation and style.

Rev. T.D. Fosbroke, *Wye Tour*, 1822

It is said that after the death of their benevolent planter, an official and officious person committed the cruel sacrilege of cutting
down some of the good man's favourite trees; immediately upon
which, there sprung up within the church, and within the very
pew he occupied, three young elm shoots, which with almost
superstitious reverence are now preserved and cherished. They
overshadow the two tall windows in that corner of the church,
and form a verdant canopy of the wonted seat of the good man.

Thomas Roscoe, *Wanderings & Excursions*, 1837

The Rector, or churchwarden having 'impiously' cut down a tree
planted by Kyrle outside, because it excluded light. The
following lines pay a pathetic tribute to the strange occurrence:-
Ye ancient elms, designed by Kyrle to wave
Your silent shadows o'er the silent grave.

J.B. Watkins, *Wye Tour*, 1896

Ross, in Monmouthshire [sic], is known chiefly as a tourist
centre and as the possessor of a church with trees growing
through its wall, but the edifice has other claims to interest than
these withered vegetable curiosities.

Edward Foord, *Cathedrals, Abbeys and Famous Churches*, 1925

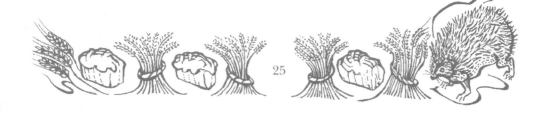

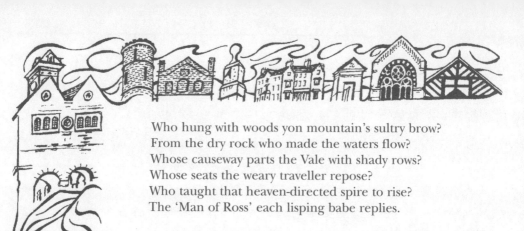

Who hung with woods yon mountain's sultry brow?
From the dry rock who made the waters flow?
Whose causeway parts the Vale with shady rows?
Whose seats the weary traveller repose?
Who taught that heaven-directed spire to rise?
The 'Man of Ross' each lisping babe replies.

Alexander Pope, 1732

A copy of this poem [above] was forwarded to Caryll in 1733, with a letter stating, 'It is not the worst poem I have written; it abounds in moral examples, for which reason it must be obnoxious in this age. God send it does any good, I really mean nothing else by writing at this time of my life.'

Pope to Caryll, *Bayfordbury MSS*

Here dwelt the 'Man of Ross'! O Traveller, hear,
Departed Merit claims a reverent tear!
Friend to the friendless, to the sick man health,
With gen'rous joy he view'd his modest wealth;
He heard the widow's heav'n-breath'd prayer of praise!
He mark'd the shelter'd orphan's tearful gaze!
And, o'er the dowry'd virgin's snowy cheek,
Bade bridal love suffuse its blushes meek!
Beneath this roof, if thy cheer'd moments pass,
Fill to the Good Man's Name one grateful Glass!
To higher zest shall MEMORY wake thy soul,
And VIRTUE mingle in th' ennobled bowl.
But if, like me, thro' life's distressful scene,
Lonely and sad thy pilgrimage hath been;
And if, thy breast with heart-sick anguish fraught,
Thou journiest onward tempest-tost in thought,
Here cheat thy cares, in gen'rous visions melt,
And dream of Goodness, thou has never felt.

S.T. Coleridge, lines written at the King's Arms,
formerly the house of The Man of Ross, 1795

Till Ross, thy charms all hearts confess'd;
Thy peaceful walks, thy hours of rest
And contemplation. Here the mind,
(Its usual luggage left behind),
Feels all its dormant fires revive,
And sees 'the Man of Ross' alive;
And hears the Twick'nham Bard again,
To KYRLE'S high virtues lift his strain;
Whose own hand cloth'd this far-fam'd hill
With rev'rend elms, that shade us still;
Whose mem'ry shall survive the day,
When elms and empires feel decay.
KYRLE die, by BARD ennobled? Never,
The Man Of Ross, shall live for ever;
And long that spire shall time defy,
To grace the flow'ry-margin'd WYE,
Scene of the morrow's joy, that prest
Its unseen beauties on our rest
In dreams; but who of dreams would tell,
Where truth sustains the song so well?

Robert Bloomfield, *The Bard of Wye*, 1813

On the floor of the chancel there is a well-preserved slab, with a simple inscription, marking the last earthly resting-place of the immortalised John Kyrle, together with that of other members of his family. Notwithstanding the sharp satire of a sentence in Pope's Ode on the Man of Ross, the plain slab was the only record of his sepulture, until one of his collateral descendants, by her will, left a sum of money to erect a monument. That on the north wall of the chancel is unskilfully done, and lacks the antiquity and imposing beauty of the grander Rudhall John Kyrle; the oval bas-relief design in the centre, surmounted with the cornucopia, is symbolical of Charity supported by Benevolence. At the base are the crest and arms of Kyrle (a chevron, with crescent at upper angle, between three fleur-de-lys), with motto, 'Virtute et Fide.' The inscription of the tablet is as follows:-

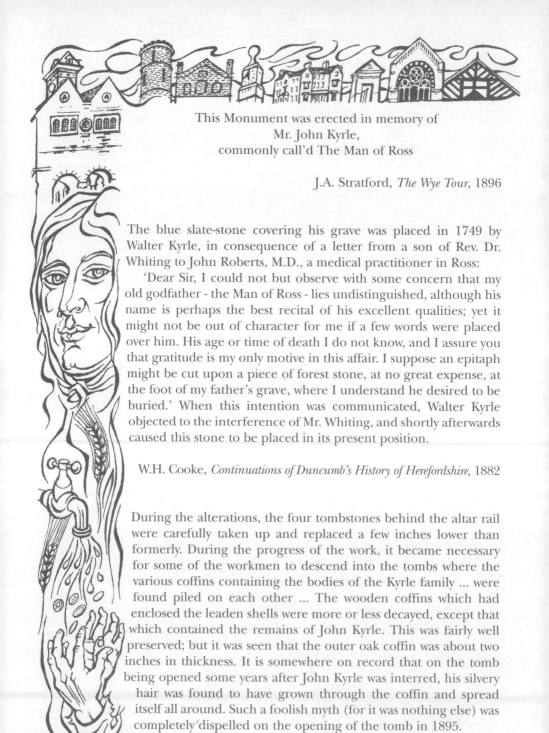

This Monument was erected in memory of
Mr. John Kyrle,
commonly call'd The Man of Ross

J.A. Stratford, *The Wye Tour*, 1896

The blue slate-stone covering his grave was placed in 1749 by Walter Kyrle, in consequence of a letter from a son of Rev. Dr. Whiting to John Roberts, M.D., a medical practitioner in Ross:
'Dear Sir, I could not but observe with some concern that my old godfather - the Man of Ross - lies undistinguished, although his name is perhaps the best recital of his excellent qualities; yet it might not be out of character for me if a few words were placed over him. His age or time of death I do not know, and I assure you that gratitude is my only motive in this affair. I suppose an epitaph might be cut upon a piece of forest stone, at no great expense, at the foot of my father's grave, where I understand he desired to be buried.' When this intention was communicated, Walter Kyrle objected to the interference of Mr. Whiting, and shortly afterwards caused this stone to be placed in its present position.

W.H. Cooke, *Continuations of Duncumb's History of Herefordshire*, 1882

During the alterations, the four tombstones behind the altar rail were carefully taken up and replaced a few inches lower than formerly. During the progress of the work, it became necessary for some of the workmen to descend into the tombs where the various coffins containing the bodies of the Kyrle family ... were found piled on each other ... The wooden coffins which had enclosed the leaden shells were more or less decayed, except that which contained the remains of John Kyrle. This was fairly well preserved; but it was seen that the outer oak coffin was about two inches in thickness. It is somewhere on record that on the tomb being opened some years after John Kyrle was interred, his silvery hair was found to have grown through the coffin and spread itself all around. Such a foolish myth (for it was nothing else) was completely dispelled on the opening of the tomb in 1895.

J.A. Stratford, *The Wye Tour*, 1896

28

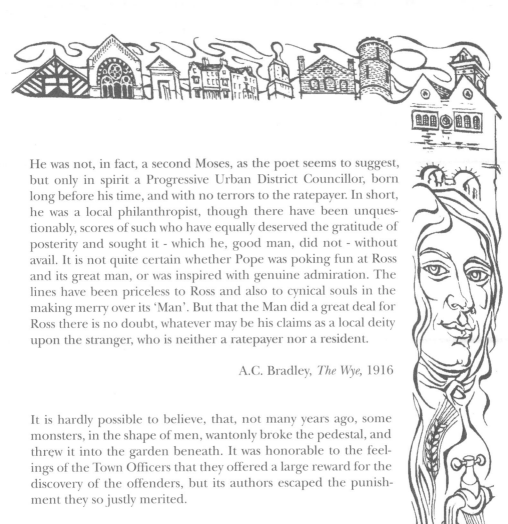

He was not, in fact, a second Moses, as the poet seems to suggest, but only in spirit a Progressive Urban District Councillor, born long before his time, and with no terrors to the ratepayer. In short, he was a local philanthropist, though there have been unquestionably, scores of such who have equally deserved the gratitude of posterity and sought it - which he, good man, did not - without avail. It is not quite certain whether Pope was poking fun at Ross and its great man, or was inspired with genuine admiration. The lines have been priceless to Ross and also to cynical souls in the making merry over its 'Man'. But that the Man did a great deal for Ross there is no doubt, whatever may be his claims as a local deity upon the stranger, who is neither a ratepayer nor a resident.

A.C. Bradley, *The Wye*, 1916

It is hardly possible to believe, that, not many years ago, some monsters, in the shape of men, wantonly broke the pedestal, and threw it into the garden beneath. It was honorable to the feelings of the Town Officers that they offered a large reward for the discovery of the offenders, but its authors escaped the punishment they so justly merited.

Charles Heath, *Excursion Down the Wye*, 1828

He died in 1724, and generations afterwards (in 1877) there was brought into being a Kyrle Society to keep his name green and encourage the love of the countryside and the planting of trees. It was formed by a group of people among whom was Octavia Hill, one of the founders of the national trust, and its work included the giving of popular concerts and the encouragement of gardening to brighten the lives of people in dull towns.

Arthur Mee, *The King's England*, 1948

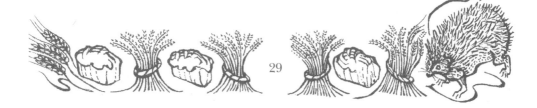

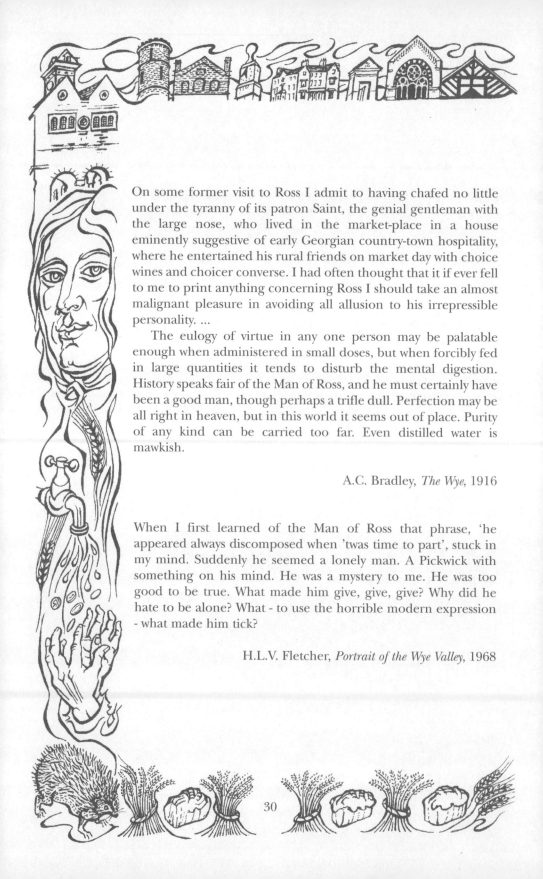

On some former visit to Ross I admit to having chafed no little under the tyranny of its patron Saint, the genial gentleman with the large nose, who lived in the market-place in a house eminently suggestive of early Georgian country-town hospitality, where he entertained his rural friends on market day with choice wines and choicer converse. I had often thought that it if ever fell to me to print anything concerning Ross I should take an almost malignant pleasure in avoiding all allusion to his irrepressible personality. ...

The eulogy of virtue in any one person may be palatable enough when administered in small doses, but when forcibly fed in large quantities it tends to disturb the mental digestion. History speaks fair of the Man of Ross, and he must certainly have been a good man, though perhaps a trifle dull. Perfection may be all right in heaven, but in this world it seems out of place. Purity of any kind can be carried too far. Even distilled water is mawkish.

A.C. Bradley, *The Wye*, 1916

When I first learned of the Man of Ross that phrase, 'he appeared always discomposed when 'twas time to part', stuck in my mind. Suddenly he seemed a lonely man. A Pickwick with something on his mind. He was a mystery to me. He was too good to be true. What made him give, give, give? Why did he hate to be alone? What - to use the horrible modern expression - what made him tick?

H.L.V. Fletcher, *Portrait of the Wye Valley*, 1968

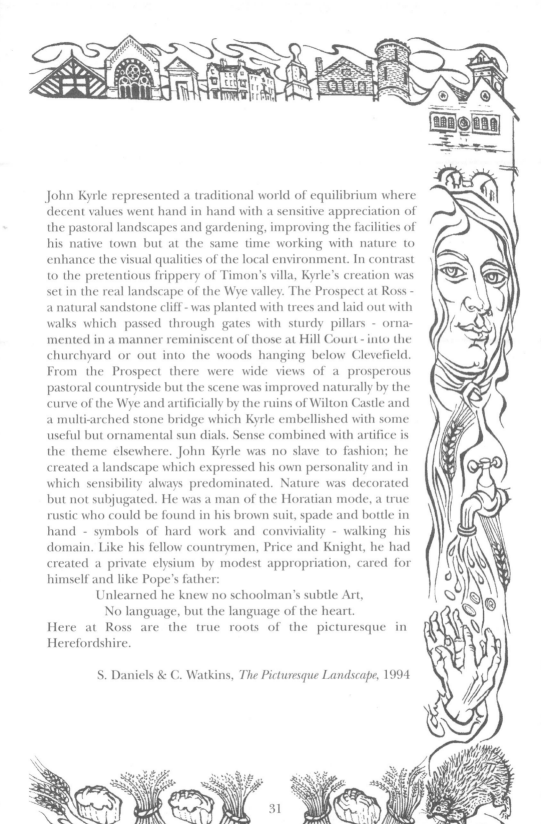

John Kyrle represented a traditional world of equilibrium where decent values went hand in hand with a sensitive appreciation of the pastoral landscapes and gardening, improving the facilities of his native town but at the same time working with nature to enhance the visual qualities of the local environment. In contrast to the pretentious frippery of Timon's villa, Kyrle's creation was set in the real landscape of the Wye valley. The Prospect at Ross - a natural sandstone cliff - was planted with trees and laid out with walks which passed through gates with sturdy pillars - ornamented in a manner reminiscent of those at Hill Court - into the churchyard or out into the woods hanging below Clevefield. From the Prospect there were wide views of a prosperous pastoral countryside but the scene was improved naturally by the curve of the Wye and artificially by the ruins of Wilton Castle and a multi-arched stone bridge which Kyrle embellished with some useful but ornamental sun dials. Sense combined with artifice is the theme elsewhere. John Kyrle was no slave to fashion; he created a landscape which expressed his own personality and in which sensibility always predominated. Nature was decorated but not subjugated. He was a man of the Horatian mode, a true rustic who could be found in his brown suit, spade and bottle in hand - symbols of hard work and conviviality - walking his domain. Like his fellow countrymen, Price and Knight, he had created a private elysium by modest appropriation, cared for himself and like Pope's father:

> Unlearned he knew no schoolman's subtle Art,
> No language, but the language of the heart.

Here at Ross are the true roots of the picturesque in Herefordshire.

S. Daniels & C. Watkins, *The Picturesque Landscape*, 1994

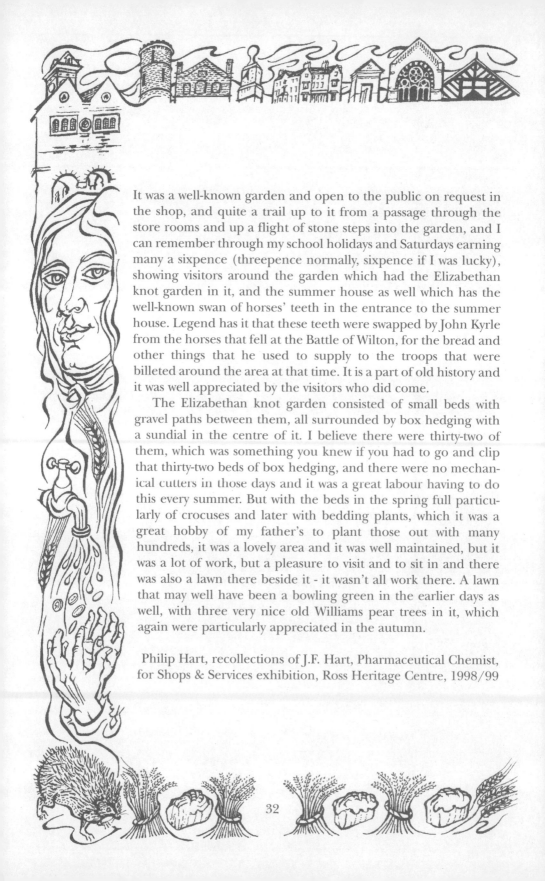

It was a well-known garden and open to the public on request in the shop, and quite a trail up to it from a passage through the store rooms and up a flight of stone steps into the garden, and I can remember through my school holidays and Saturdays earning many a sixpence (threepence normally, sixpence if I was lucky), showing visitors around the garden which had the Elizabethan knot garden in it, and the summer house as well which has the well-known swan of horses' teeth in the entrance to the summer house. Legend has it that these teeth were swapped by John Kyrle from the horses that fell at the Battle of Wilton, for the bread and other things that he used to supply to the troops that were billeted around the area at that time. It is a part of old history and it was well appreciated by the visitors who did come.

The Elizabethan knot garden consisted of small beds with gravel paths between them, all surrounded by box hedging with a sundial in the centre of it. I believe there were thirty-two of them, which was something you knew if you had to go and clip that thirty-two beds of box hedging, and there were no mechanical cutters in those days and it was a great labour having to do this every summer. But with the beds in the spring full particularly of crocuses and later with bedding plants, which it was a great hobby of my father's to plant those out with many hundreds, it was a lovely area and it was well maintained, but it was a lot of work, but a pleasure to visit and to sit in and there was also a lawn there beside it - it wasn't all work there. A lawn that may well have been a bowling green in the earlier days as well, with three very nice old Williams pear trees in it, which again were particularly appreciated in the autumn.

Philip Hart, recollections of J.F. Hart, Pharmaceutical Chemist, for Shops & Services exhibition, Ross Heritage Centre, 1998/99

THE PROSPECT

Indenture between John Kyrle and William Fisher of Ross, innkeeper. Lease from Mr. Kyrle of Bishops Court to William Fisher.

... John Kyrle at the taking of the said lease did and still doth intend his workmen to enter upon the said land called Bishops Court to set out same into walks and to plant rows of trees and raise grass plots therein and also to build all such buildings walks hedges fences ditches and other ornaments as he or they should think fit or devise to make the same a Publick walking place. And further to do any other matter or thing whatsoever as he or they should think fit or devise in or for the making and continuing same as a Publick Walking place during the whole term thereinafter granted and also liberty for all and every Person and Inhabitant of the Town of Ross and all and every other Person whatsoever from time to time and at all times during the said demise to enter and have free ingress and egress to from and in the said land called Bishops Court as well as for their Walking and diversion as also for the Whitening and drying of linen Clothes upon the grass plots and hedges there without leave or license of or paying or rendering any recompense or reward whatsoever.

The said William Fisher not to erect any buildings Stanks Stacks Rocks Privy house pigs cott Stalls or pens for pigs or plant any Tree or trees hedge or hedges whatsoever in Bishops Court or Bishops Court Bank or do any matter or thing that may annoy or incommode or be a nuisance to the said Walks or the Prospect or pleasantness thereof.

Not to turn or suffer to be turned in Beasts or Swine into Bishops Court but graze same with sheep only and the soil and dung of such sheep to be spread thereon.

To seed the grass until same be made clean and free from weeds.

To mow down the grass which by the staining of said Sheep shall be standing higher than other parts thereof.

signed 24th Dec. 1713. Deed poll under the hand and seal of John Kyrle, 3rd May 1696

Seated some years ago in the spacious Alcove, apparently here erected for social pleasure by Mr. Kyrle, at the upper end of this fine piece of ground, with the late Mr. Thomas Hopkins of Ross, he informed me, that one day in the week, in the summer season, this Green was the resort of the principal gentlemen of the Town and neighbourhood, and that he had seen thirty persons of the first consequence (dressed in their rich scarlet gold laced waistcoats) enjoying its amusement, - and that when he was a boy (the period to which he alluded), it was considered 'a great mark of favor the being permitted to witness, from the top of the wall, that then inclosed it, the persons who were thus engaged.' These remarks were more strongly called forth, from his seeing two menials of the Inn, with some beer in their hands, indulging in the same recreation....

... its beautiful situation; from whence you enjoy a charming view of the country, and particularly of the river, which meanders ... through meadows of the richest verdure. In the centre of this field was a FOUNTAIN, which supplied the near inhabitants with water; but, for its becoming a receptacle for the carcases of dead animals, it was afterwards disused. William Dobles described it as forming an oval of some extent, in proportion to its depth, which was near eight feet, the sides secured with brick, and the bottom paved with fine square stones. He did not remember it when FILLED WITH WATER, but his father had often mentioned and described it to him. When a boy, he used to play at marbles in it, and at last they took the pavement away to rear the balls on, when they played at fives in the churchyard. It was filled up in the year 1794, so that its memory is preserved only by tradition.

... the reason for suffering the Fountain to be neglected, originated in the frequent bursting of the pipes, by throwing up the water to such an amazing height, which occasioned infinite trouble and expense to keep them in repair.

Charles Heath, *Excursion Down the Wye from Ross to Monmouth*, 1799

Rofs ftands high, and commands many diftant views; but that from the church-yard is the moft admired; and is indeed very amufing. It confifts of an eafy fweep of the Wye; and of an extenfive country beyond it. But it is not picturefque. It is marked by no characteriftic objects: it is broken into too many parts; and it is feen from too high a point.

William Gilpin, *Observations of the River Wye*, 1793

34

The scene is rich and pleasant, but there are no striking features to fix the attention. Immediately beneath the Wye sweeps in, in a semi-circular form. Upon the river I counted five pleasure boats laying ready for Passengers.

Joseph Farrington's *Diaries*, 1803

The view from hence is a fine relief from the dark brick buildings and awkward streets of the town. If the eye limits itself to the horse-shoe curve of the river, the green meadow, the ivied towers of Wilton Castle, and the light Bridge, there is a very pleasing though rather formal and somewhat of a Dutch Landscape.

Rev. T.D. Fosbroke, *Wye Tour*, 1826

Gaze with delight on one of the most quietly beautiful landscapes in England - whose smooth green eminences, gentle groves, orchards and hop plantations (the latter far finer objects than the vineyards of the continent), white cottages, villages, and village spires, give an endless and yet simple variety to the picture.

Leith Ritchie, *Narrative of a Pedestrian Ramble*, 1839

... in or about the year 1838 James Barrett took down the buildings on said premises and rebuilt upon part of the site of said Freehold heriditaments called the Pounds otherwise Bishops Court an Hotel since called Barretts Royal Hotel with Coachhouses Stables and other buildings for the use and convenience of said Hotel and also erected and built on other part of said Freehold premises called the Points otherwise Bishops Court a Dwellinghouse or building which has since been used as a Tap to said Hotel and called the Royal Hotel Tap. J. Barrett also laid out the said piece or parcel of Land called Bishops Court otherwise the Prospect and part of Bishops Court Bank into Gardens and Pleasure Grounds and formed Walks therein and otherwise beau-tified and improved the same.

Explanation of the Abstracts of Title to the Royal Hotel, 1860

In the evening many persons were assembled on the Prospect, but we did not hear that any damage was committed. It was said that a quantity of oil had been poured upon the seats and in different places, which was conjectured to be the work of Mr. Barrett's servants. Very considerable excitement prevailed in Ross, and groups of persons were continually strolling about the streets and on to the Prospect.

Hereford Journal, Friday 14th July, 1848

Serious rioting and destruction of property at Ross. The 12th July will ever be a memorable day in Ross....

On Monday the place was the scene of great attraction, and it was easy to perceive that a row was brewing.

Soon after 6 o'clock, a signal was given for the work of destruction to commence, and very soon the peas, beans, potatoes, and cabbage plants were strewed and trampled about the ground, amidst the cheers of the hundreds of spectators who were present by that time. Many of the handsome plants in the ornamental portion of the grounds next fell victim to the fury of the mob. The gates attached to these gardens had all been thrown open during the day by the instructions of the hotel managers, thus giving the public the right to free ingress and egress, and the inhabitants, we need hardly say, made the most liberal use of the privilege. The members of the Barrel Friendly Society (who were celebrating their anniversary that day) took the opportunity thus afforded them of marching round the gardens, headed by the Trafalgar band, after leaving church in the morning.

The next grand move was an attack upon the billiard-room, which, it is said, is built upon public land. The doors of the room had been previously locked, and Mr. Henry Minett, acting on behalf of the hotel company, endeavoured to pacify the crowd, and to prevent an entry being forced into the place. For some time he stood his ground, but ultimately the besiegers obtained a victory by strategy, and burst open the door, smashed the ornamental window to splinters, and so took this means of asserting their right. One of the most active of the party mounted the billiard table and delivered an address - The lavatory adjoining the billiard room was soon peopled with a mixed assembly, and ablutions were indulged in - and were certainly in some cases very necessary - by those who felt so disposed... The crowning act then commenced at the kitchen garden we have previously referred to. The beansticks and other inflammable articles were piled up and set on fire in the hedge at the corner next the churchyard, close by the ivy-grown stone gateway, which, happily, was not in any way injured by the fire. Fresh fuel was added to the burning mass, so arranged as to carry the fire along the length of the hedge, loud bursts of cheering made the place resound again. Axes were next set to work, and all the doors, gates, and posts, leading from the garden of the hotel grounds, were broken up by willing hands and cast to the flames, which, mounting higher and higher, threw a lurid reflection around, lighting up the church tower and other objects in the vicinity of the Prospect. Water-butts - in fact everything that would burn - were torn from their places, brought along to the spot where the wholesale destruction was going on, and soon converted into ashes. The hedges all round were afterwards fired at different places, and there are no less then 12 distinct places where a fire had been kindled and shrubs and hedges more or less destroyed. This sort of work went on till long after midnight; but gradually the place was cleared - a smart shower of rain ensuing.

In the morning a truly piteous scene exhibited itself. Every gate was found to have been taken away and destroyed, and all the gateposts, except a few which had been so firmly fixed as to defy all efforts to remove them, had met with the same fate... Nearly all the flower beds were in ruins, and the gravel paths strewn with the debris. Flower pots had been overturned, and flower stands and terracotta vases lay kicked and smashed on the lawns. In the grotto, to which, we believe, the public lay no claim, the fibre-wainscoting had been torn down from the walls, the seats pulled up, the stone-work demolished, and the place abused in every conceivable way. Two broken panes in the upper windows of the hotel showed the busy handiwork of some one anxious to do a little on the quiet. The billiard-room and lavatory was in a most dirty state from the immense traffic that had taken place in so short a time. Passing round to the back of the billiard-room, there is another kitchen garden used as a drying ground. A greenhouse is here fixed, with the glass of which great havoc has been made.

During all the time the work of destruction was going on, the police, though near at hand, remained aloof. The question being that of a disputed right of way, they considered it beyond their province to interfere, while the row was confined to the public part of the grounds. This, undoubtedly, was a very wise step, for with the very small body of men under his charge, the superintendent would have been unable to do anything except increase the commotion and perhaps lead to something more serious. The chief amount of the damage, however, was done by several scores of boys and a few labourers and mechanics, the more respectable portion of the crowd remaining aloof, encouraging the others by their laughter and cheers.

Early on Tuesday morning, Capt. Telfer ... came to Ross in company with Supt. Wilson and other officers of the force, and during the day a posse of constables, armed with cutlasses, were dispatched from Hereford to Ross, and in the evening were stationed in little squads at various parts of the grounds. No molestation was offered by any of the constabulary force towards the visitors who continued to pour in and to roam about at will. We have no hesitation in protesting against the cutlasses, for we are sure that the presence of the police would have been sufficient to deter anyone from committing violence... In fact, remembering that a large proportion of the visitors to the grounds were respectable tradesmen and their wives, who we presume can feel equally warm in asserting their rights - though in a more dignified manner - as the roughest of roughs; we cannot do less than denounce the cutlasses (especially as they were not introduced till after all the damage was done) as an insult to our town and its inhabitants...

Although great numbers assembled in the Prospect in the evening, there was no attempt at a renewal of the previous night's performances. Various speeches were delivered, all bearing upon the right of the people to the Prospect. Pope's famous ode which immortalised John Kyrle - now dearer in the heart of every Ross man than ever - was several times recited. As night drew on the numbers decreased and quietude began to reign. The next morning the police went back to Hereford. Warrants were issued for the apprehension of those who had made themselves the most conspicuous the preceding night, and several arrests made...

Ross Gazette, Thursday 15th July, 1869

On Wednesday night there was a furious contest for possession of the right of walking on the Lower Garden, Mr. Barrett and his servants being arrayed on the one side, and numbers of the inhabitants, headed by respectable individuals, on the other. Mr.

Barrett, who appears to have been roughly handled, maintained his position for four hours, and saw the crowd disperse. Among the parties implicated in the alleged riot on Wednesday were, Mr. James, surgeon, Mr. Powell, chymist, Mr. R. Powle, etc., etc. On Thursday night the crowd assembled was much more numerous than before, but Mr. Barrett offering no opposition, and the gate which had been newly-erected during the day, being left open, allowed free access to all part of the pleasure grounds. After perambulating the walks for about two hours the assemblance quietly dispersed without doing any material injury. A large body of constables, regular and special, were in attendance, but, happily, their services were not required.

Hereford Journal, Wednesday 19th July, 1848

On Thursday evening the band of the Ross Rifle Volunteers played in the Prospect. A large concourse of respectable persons was attracted to the spot, and the proceedings were very orderly. The scene, in fact, presented a gay and animated appearance, and the performance of the band gave much satisfaction. Several operatic selections, etc., were played in such a manner as to denote that the band is rapidly improving. We hope that the public will not only support the movement, but, if requisite, subscribe in a liberal manner towards the purchase of new music and instruments, so as to render 'the People's Band' - if we may so term it - all that can be desired in strength and efficiency.

Ross Gazette Supplement, Thursday 29th July, 1869

Ross Prospect. On Thursday morning last, the hedges (or rather the remains of them) which previously to last July enclosed the piece of garden ground forming a portion of the Prospect, were rooted up by a few labourers, under the supervision of J.H. Skyrme Esq., and by night-time the whole of the bushes were 'grubbed-up' and removed. It is intended in the autumn to fill in the hollow space in the centre and to make the Prospect perfectly level, which will effect a decided improvement. By this means the Prospect or the chief portion of it, will be secured to the town of Ross for ever - Hooray!!

Ross Gazette, Thursday 21st April, 1870

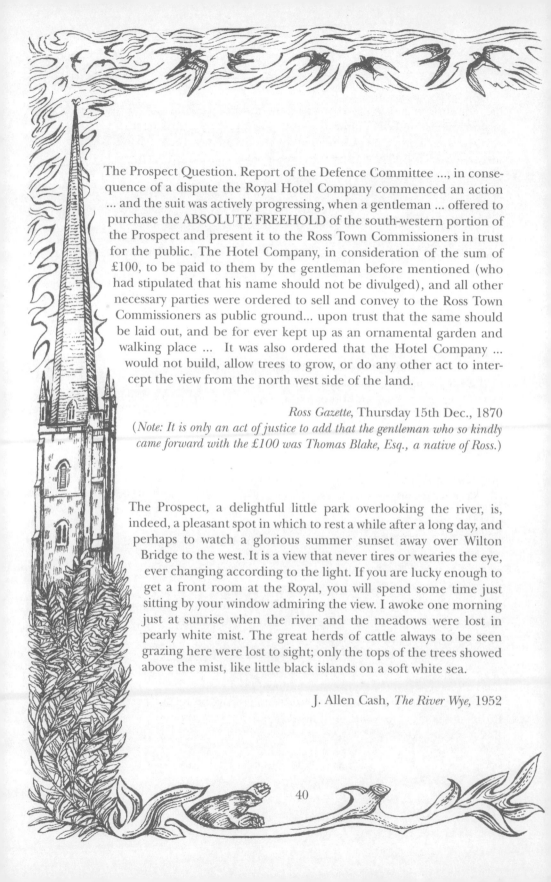

The Prospect Question. Report of the Defence Committee ..., in consequence of a dispute the Royal Hotel Company commenced an action ... and the suit was actively progressing, when a gentleman ... offered to purchase the ABSOLUTE FREEHOLD of the south-western portion of the Prospect and present it to the Ross Town Commissioners in trust for the public. The Hotel Company, in consideration of the sum of £100, to be paid to them by the gentleman before mentioned (who had stipulated that his name should not be divulged), and all other necessary parties were ordered to sell and convey to the Ross Town Commissioners as public ground... upon trust that the same should be laid out, and be for ever kept up as an ornamental garden and walking place ... It was also ordered that the Hotel Company ... would not build, allow trees to grow, or do any other act to intercept the view from the north west side of the land.

Ross Gazette, Thursday 15th Dec., 1870
(*Note: It is only an act of justice to add that the gentleman who so kindly came forward with the £100 was Thomas Blake, Esq., a native of Ross.*)

The Prospect, a delightful little park overlooking the river, is, indeed, a pleasant spot in which to rest a while after a long day, and perhaps to watch a glorious summer sunset away over Wilton Bridge to the west. It is a view that never tires or wearies the eye, ever changing according to the light. If you are lucky enough to get a front room at the Royal, you will spend some time just sitting by your window admiring the view. I awoke one morning just at sunrise when the river and the meadows were lost in pearly white mist. The great herds of cattle always to be seen grazing here were lost to sight; only the tops of the trees showed above the mist, like little black islands on a soft white sea.

J. Allen Cash, *The River Wye*, 1952

THE TOWN

The annals of this town record no events of eminent historical interest.

Paterson's Roads, 1826

Nothin' Goes in Ross.

old saying

Ross is an old fashioned town, but it is very beautifully situated, and if there is little finery in the appearance of the inhabitants, there is also little misery.

William Cobbett, *Rural Rides*, 1830

Ross was made by the same King [Stephen] a 'free Borough', but not incorporated by Charter. In 1305, its inhabitants were required to return two Burgesses to the Parliament, summoned to meet at Westminster, and Adam de la More and Thomas le Mercer were the Members returned; since that period no writ has been addressed to this Borough for the exercise of similar responsibility. The government of the town was during many centuries in the appointees of the Manor Court, viz. a mayor, or sergeant at mace, and four constables, but the jurisdiction of such officials has ceased, and the government of the town is vested in Commissioners elected by the ratepayers under the provisions of 'The Ross Improvement Act of 1865.'

W.H. Cooke, *Continuations of Duncumb's History of Herefordshire*, 1882

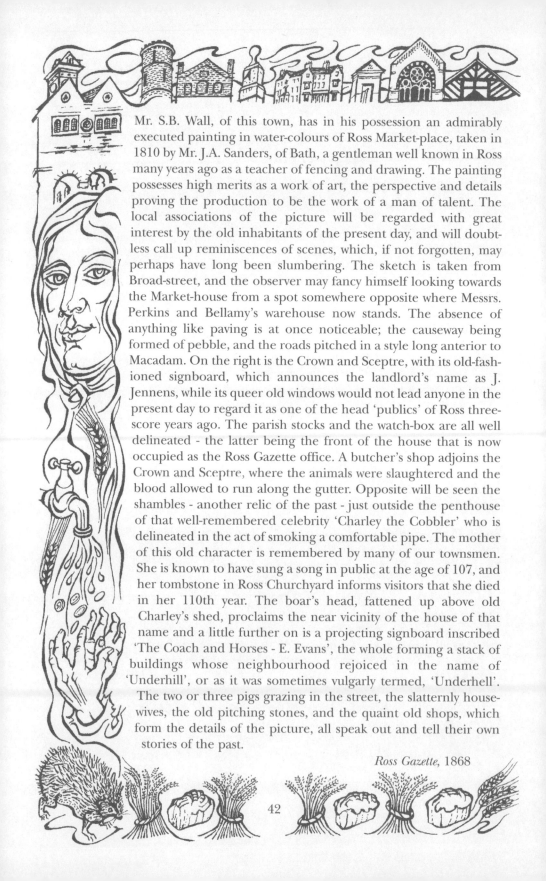

Mr. S.B. Wall, of this town, has in his possession an admirably executed painting in water-colours of Ross Market-place, taken in 1810 by Mr. J.A. Sanders, of Bath, a gentleman well known in Ross many years ago as a teacher of fencing and drawing. The painting possesses high merits as a work of art, the perspective and details proving the production to be the work of a man of talent. The local associations of the picture will be regarded with great interest by the old inhabitants of the present day, and will doubtless call up reminiscences of scenes, which, if not forgotten, may perhaps have long been slumbering. The sketch is taken from Broad-street, and the observer may fancy himself looking towards the Market-house from a spot somewhere opposite where Messrs. Perkins and Bellamy's warehouse now stands. The absence of anything like paving is at once noticeable; the causeway being formed of pebble, and the roads pitched in a style long anterior to Macadam. On the right is the Crown and Sceptre, with its old-fashioned signboard, which announces the landlord's name as J. Jennens, while its queer old windows would not lead anyone in the present day to regard it as one of the head 'publics' of Ross three-score years ago. The parish stocks and the watch-box are all well delineated - the latter being the front of the house that is now occupied as the Ross Gazette office. A butcher's shop adjoins the Crown and Sceptre, where the animals were slaughtered and the blood allowed to run along the gutter. Opposite will be seen the shambles - another relic of the past - just outside the penthouse of that well-remembered celebrity 'Charley the Cobbler' who is delineated in the act of smoking a comfortable pipe. The mother of this old character is remembered by many of our townsmen. She is known to have sung a song in public at the age of 107, and her tombstone in Ross Churchyard informs visitors that she died in her 110th year. The boar's head, fattened up above old Charley's shed, proclaims the near vicinity of the house of that name and a little further on is a projecting signboard inscribed 'The Coach and Horses - E. Evans', the whole forming a stack of buildings whose neighbourhood rejoiced in the name of 'Underhill', or as it was sometimes vulgarly termed, 'Underhell'. The two or three pigs grazing in the street, the slatternly housewives, the old pitching stones, and the quaint old shops, which form the details of the picture, all speak out and tell their own stories of the past.

Ross Gazette, 1868

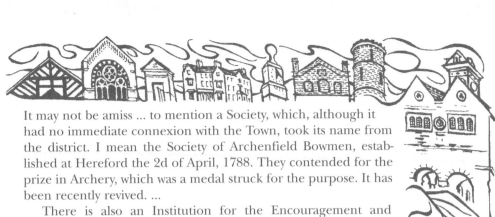

It may not be amiss ... to mention a Society, which, although it had no immediate connexion with the Town, took its name from the district. I mean the Society of Archenfield Bowmen, established at Hereford the 2d of April, 1788. They contended for the prize in Archery, which was a medal struck for the purpose. It has been recently revived. ...

There is also an Institution for the Encouragement and Benefit of faithful Female Servants. ...

A permanent Library for the purpose of forming a valuable collection of works of high taste and standard character was established at Ross, chiefly by the exertions of W. Hooper, Esq., the Rev. Mr. Fosbroke, &c. In 1817 above a hundred volumes was contributed by the members, in order that fine works may be purchased at the outset. Every subscriber has the power of ordering any work he chooses, but must take to them at the expiration of the year, when all the books are sold, at a certain reduced price, if no one be inclined to bid higher; this stipulation is thought sufficient to prevent the introduction of improper works.

T.B. Watkins, *The Ross Guide*, 1827

Ross, at this moment, I hear from the most respectable of its inhabitants, is fuller of bad characters and prostitutes than ever known before.

Extract from a letter to the editor entitled 'County Wakes and the New Police' from 'A Willing Subscriber.' *Hereford Journal*, Wednesday 3rd Jan., 1838

The long walks around Ross, though including very fine prospects, will not here be mentioned; only those within a distance, to which females would not object.

Rev. T.A. Fosbroke, *Wye Tour*, 1822
Note: The Rev. Fosbroke, vicar of Walford, suggested that what Ross needed was better lodging houses, more billiard tables, and 'a public gaudy galley'.

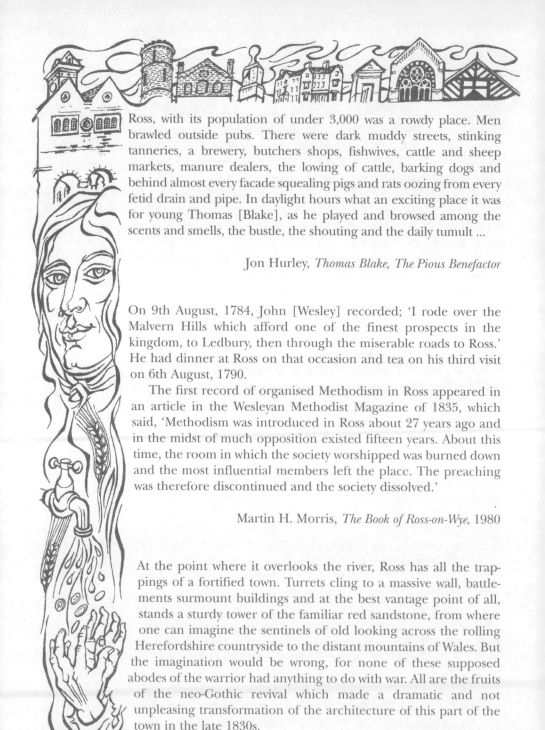

Ross, with its population of under 3,000 was a rowdy place. Men brawled outside pubs. There were dark muddy streets, stinking tanneries, a brewery, butchers shops, fishwives, cattle and sheep markets, manure dealers, the lowing of cattle, barking dogs and behind almost every facade squealing pigs and rats oozing from every fetid drain and pipe. In daylight hours what an exciting place it was for young Thomas [Blake], as he played and browsed among the scents and smells, the bustle, the shouting and the daily tumult ...

Jon Hurley, *Thomas Blake, The Pious Benefactor*

On 9th August, 1784, John [Wesley] recorded; 'I rode over the Malvern Hills which afford one of the finest prospects in the kingdom, to Ledbury, then through the miserable roads to Ross.' He had dinner at Ross on that occasion and tea on his third visit on 6th August, 1790.

The first record of organised Methodism in Ross appeared in an article in the Wesleyan Methodist Magazine of 1835, which said, 'Methodism was introduced in Ross about 27 years ago and in the midst of much opposition existed fifteen years. About this time, the room in which the society worshipped was burned down and the most influential members left the place. The preaching was therefore discontinued and the society dissolved.'

Martin H. Morris, *The Book of Ross-on-Wye*, 1980

At the point where it overlooks the river, Ross has all the trappings of a fortified town. Turrets cling to a massive wall, battlements surmount buildings and at the best vantage point of all, stands a sturdy tower of the familiar red sandstone, from where one can imagine the sentinels of old looking across the rolling Herefordshire countryside to the distant mountains of Wales. But the imagination would be wrong, for none of these supposed abodes of the warrior had anything to do with war. All are the fruits of the neo-Gothic revival which made a dramatic and not unpleasing transformation of the architecture of this part of the town in the late 1830s.

Martin H. Morris, *The Book of Ross-on-Wye*, 1980

At my visit to this Workhouse today, I saw all those classed here of unsound mind; they are five women, one of whom only was in bed, and but for slight disposition. This house is still overcrowded and the means at the disposal of the Master and Matron for securing the personal cleanliness of the inmates inadequate. For 120 inmates of whom 60 are children, there is one portable bath; the only other bath is that in the receiving ward. This necessitates I am told 10 persons being washed weekly in the same water - a most objectionable practice. The house diet, giving only 3oz. of solid meat in 3 days of the week, is too low for persons classed as insane and extra diet should be given to all of them. I learnt that there was no closet for either of the female sick wards. The dress supplied is sufficient - I trust that when the additions to this Workhouse, too long delayed, but now in progress, shall be completed, the imbecile class may be accommodated in the infirmary, as far as possible, that there they may have fixed baths with hot and cold water supply pipes. The bedding which I inspected was clean but under blankets are required. The ground for exercise is, it seems, limited temporarily by the building operations; the imbeciles capable of walking abroad should I think, be frequently taken beyond the premises.

C.A. Virginia Morgan, *The Ross Union Workhouse* (April 1873)

Ross is famous for the longevity of its inhabitants, who are healthy as well as long-lived.

The writer, accidentally meeting with the Registrar's return of the mortality of Ross for January, 1874, found the number of deaths were 14, five of the persons having attained the ages respectively of 70, 71, 78, 82, and 83.

During the past twelvemonth, the death registry of one of the medical officers of Ross contains the names of 40 persons who have died in his district, whose united ages amount to 2,201, being an average of 54 years. One was 99, and another 95. Eight were over 80, eight over 70, three over 60, five over 50; one between 40 and 50; four between 30 and 40; one between 20 and 30; and eight under 20, of whom five were infants under 12 months, and two under two years.

Ross Gazette, August 1879

During the past fortnight six persons died in Ross (five of them in the workhouse), whose united ages amounted to 491 years, exclusive of the odd months. With these the average was nearly 83.

Ross Gazette, June 12th, 1890

The town today, though much modernized of late by the erection of new buildings, and by the numerous handsome plate-glass fronts which have been put in several shops and places of business, has still a somewhat antiquated and old-world appearance, and presents in this respect a great contrast to the melancholy uniformity of many modern towns. This does not, however, apply to the style and manner of conducting business, which is thoroughly up-to-date, both as to the quality and selection of articles offered for sale.

Edward J. Burrow, *Wye Valley Illustrated Guide*, 1905

Some years ago a cute trick was played by a couple of nomadic Steeple Jacks, who caused a scare by stating that they had discovered on inspecting other churches, that the copper conductor, by being let into the capstone instead of being isolated and carried outside it, would be the means of conveying the electric fluid into the building instead of carrying it down to the outer earth. They suggested that such was the case here. Having obtained permission to inspect the summit, they borrowed all the long ladders they could get hold of and attached them to the spire, from tower to weathercock. During their temporary absence, however, a plucky individual ascended the ladders and examined the capstone. He found the conductor properly placed, and that there was not the slightest danger. The Steeple Jacks then defiantly refused to take down the ladders (difficult and dangerous work) until they were paid a pretty good sum - we think it was £10. As they were 'masters of the situation', there was no alternative but to make the best of the matter; so, after a little haggling, they were paid off indignantly. It was afterwards found out that the 'sell' had been successfully practised in other towns besides Ross.

J.A. Stratford, *The Wye Tour*, 1896

Owing to the situation of the Town, which is upon a rock, there are very few pumps, and it is principally supplied with water by an engine, which, by means of pipes, furnishes every house with an abundant quantity, at a reasonable rate. There are also plugs in the streets, in case of fire.

T.B. Watkins, *The Ross Guide*, 1827

With the comparative cheapness of property, it is an inducement both to the tourist to make it his stopping place, and to those who are looking for a permanent abiding-place to settle down as residents. The water supply is excellent, and the town being built on a steep slope above the river, the drainage system is well arranged, and there is no fear of dampness.

Edward J. Burrow, *Wye Valley Illustrated Guide*, 1905

Ross, being increasingly looked upon as an inland holiday resort, it will be well that our visitors should know how they are catered for from a health point of view. Our sewerage system, at considerable cost, has been rendered well nigh perfect, and further improvements are contemplated.

Alfred Greer, *Ross, the River Wye & the Forest of Dean*, 1947

Many houses relied on wells, and when in 1859 the Commissioners placed an iron drinking bowl at the public pump at the Market Place, the water there was described as the best in town. For two decades the Commissioners discussed the water supply. In 1880 they were told that 353 of the 792 houses in the town had no water, 126 received the river supply and 19 were on a supply provided by Joseph Turnock from a lake at his house at Merrivale.

The problem was eventually solved by Thomas Blake, who in 1887 provided a wholesome supply from the artesian wells at Alton Court, which was pumped to the reservoir on Penyard before going by gravitation to the entire town. The soft

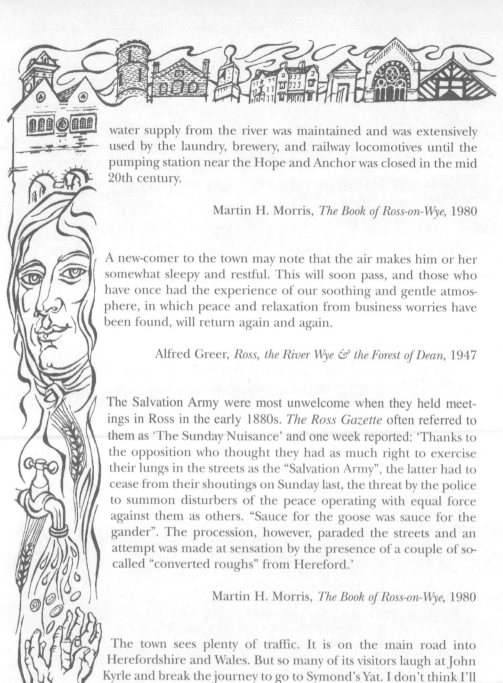

water supply from the river was maintained and was extensively used by the laundry, brewery, and railway locomotives until the pumping station near the Hope and Anchor was closed in the mid 20th century.

Martin H. Morris, *The Book of Ross-on-Wye*, 1980

A new-comer to the town may note that the air makes him or her somewhat sleepy and restful. This will soon pass, and those who have once had the experience of our soothing and gentle atmosphere, in which peace and relaxation from business worries have been found, will return again and again.

Alfred Greer, *Ross, the River Wye & the Forest of Dean*, 1947

The Salvation Army were most unwelcome when they held meetings in Ross in the early 1880s. *The Ross Gazette* often referred to them as 'The Sunday Nuisance' and one week reported: 'Thanks to the opposition who thought they had as much right to exercise their lungs in the streets as the "Salvation Army", the latter had to cease from their shoutings on Sunday last, the threat by the police to summon disturbers of the peace operating with equal force against them as others. "Sauce for the goose was sauce for the gander". The procession, however, paraded the streets and an attempt was made at sensation by the presence of a couple of so-called "converted roughs" from Hereford.'

Martin H. Morris, *The Book of Ross-on-Wye*, 1980

The town sees plenty of traffic. It is on the main road into Herefordshire and Wales. But so many of its visitors laugh at John Kyrle and break the journey to go to Symond's Yat. I don't think I'll go there after all.

H.L.V. Fletcher, *Portrait of the Wye Valley*, 1968

It was in a little alley, off which were five or six of ... small dwellings. They each had only one door and were dark and dirty. The floors were of stone. There seemed to be just one central pump which they all had to use for their drinking water and for washing themselves and their clothes. There was one communal 'privy'. The people were fearfully poor and the life there must have been dreadful. The family I had gone to see; mother, father, son and daughter, were in a bad way, for the only occupation the father had was in using his little 'go-cart'. In this truck he would fetch things for people and those who were sorry for him would engage him to transport small items. He would carry coke from the gas works and do any jobs he could get that would earn him a copper or two. The woman was dirty and it was said that she had been born in the corner of a field at hop picking time. Others said that she was of gypsy stock, but I do not think that this was so, though she was certainly very dark and had beautiful curly black hair. Her little girl was seldom fully clothed. I never saw her with shoes on and she was usually covered with only a shift type of dress. My sympathetic mother provided her with knickers from time to time, but these were never in use for long. We came to the conclusion that they were sold and the money used in other ways.

Jessie M. Stonham, *Daughter of Wyedean & Kernow*, 1978

Not far from the market were the worst slums of Ross. They were in Brampton Street and Overross Street and when we were taken for walks which involved passing through these streets we had to keep to the middle of the road. The people would often come out fighting and screaming, the women tearing one another's hair and the men shouting, kicking and punching. They were, for the most part, dirty and unkempt, ill clothed and illmannered. They would throw out their refuse and it was not uncommon to see a woman coming out with a bucket of dirty water or swill and throw it straight out into the road. The contents of teapots and of chamberpots were dealt with in the same way and could hit folk passing by if they failed to keep out of the way.

Jessie M. Stonham, *Daughter of Wyedean & Kernow*, 1978

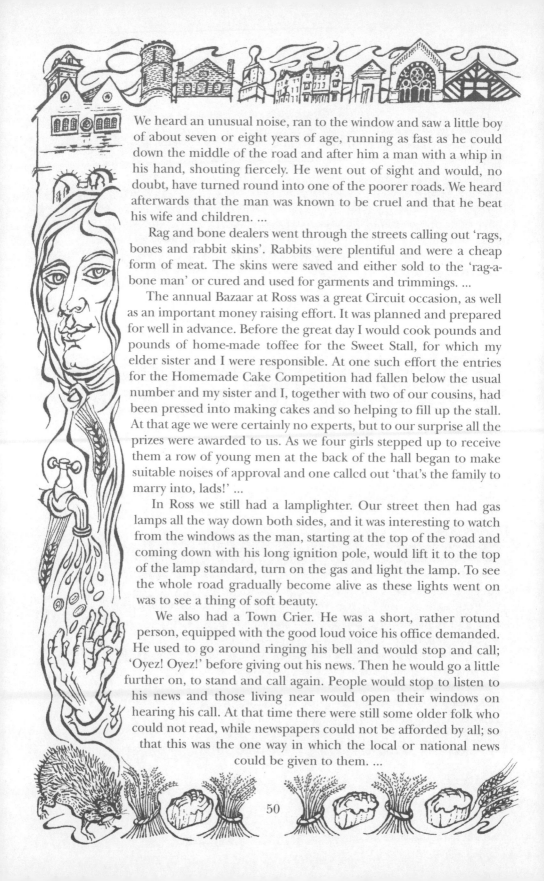

We heard an unusual noise, ran to the window and saw a little boy of about seven or eight years of age, running as fast as he could down the middle of the road and after him a man with a whip in his hand, shouting fiercely. He went out of sight and would, no doubt, have turned round into one of the poorer roads. We heard afterwards that the man was known to be cruel and that he beat his wife and children. ...

Rag and bone dealers went through the streets calling out 'rags, bones and rabbit skins'. Rabbits were plentiful and were a cheap form of meat. The skins were saved and either sold to the 'rag-a-bone man' or cured and used for garments and trimmings. ...

The annual Bazaar at Ross was a great Circuit occasion, as well as an important money raising effort. It was planned and prepared for well in advance. Before the great day I would cook pounds and pounds of home-made toffee for the Sweet Stall, for which my elder sister and I were responsible. At one such effort the entries for the Homemade Cake Competition had fallen below the usual number and my sister and I, together with two of our cousins, had been pressed into making cakes and so helping to fill up the stall. At that age we were certainly no experts, but to our surprise all the prizes were awarded to us. As we four girls stepped up to receive them a row of young men at the back of the hall began to make suitable noises of approval and one called out 'that's the family to marry into, lads!' ...

In Ross we still had a lamplighter. Our street then had gas lamps all the way down both sides, and it was interesting to watch from the windows as the man, starting at the top of the road and coming down with his long ignition pole, would lift it to the top of the lamp standard, turn on the gas and light the lamp. To see the whole road gradually become alive as these lights went on was to see a thing of soft beauty.

We also had a Town Crier. He was a short, rather rotund person, equipped with the good loud voice his office demanded. He used to go around ringing his bell and would stop and call; 'Oyez! Oyez!' before giving out his news. Then he would go a little further on, to stand and call again. People would stop to listen to his news and those living near would open their windows on hearing his call. At that time there were still some older folk who could not read, while newspapers could not be afforded by all; so that this was the one way in which the local or national news could be given to them. ...

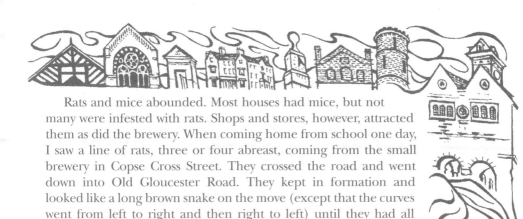

Rats and mice abounded. Most houses had mice, but not many were infested with rats. Shops and stores, however, attracted them as did the brewery. When coming home from school one day, I saw a line of rats, three or four abreast, coming from the small brewery in Copse Cross Street. They crossed the road and went down into Old Gloucester Road. They kept in formation and looked like a long brown snake on the move (except that the curves went from left to right and then right to left) until they had all crossed the road safely. I was not the only one watching this unusual and rather horrifying spectacle. I have never seen rats in formation and in such numbers since and have often wondered why they were moving out and where they were going. ...

I frequently saw [the workhouse's] younger male inmates working in the gardens (which were opposite and occupied a triangular site bordered by Alton Street and Sussex and Kent Avenues) and its older ones sitting on upright seats in their uniform clothes, the ladies with white starched aprons and bonnets and their hands folded in their laps. They seemed always to be in the same straight-backed, yet abject, position which spoke of their terminal outlook.

Jessie M. Stonham, *Daughter of Wyedean & Kernow*, 1978

Ross-on-Wye has an annual average rainfall (based on a record dating back to 1818) of only $28^{1}/_{3}$ inches, which is low for a town situated in Western England. The geographical position of Ross is answerable for this happy circumstance, as the town lies in what is called a 'rain-shadow' caused by the presence of high hills and mountains to southwestward and westward (the Abergavenny Heights and the Black Mountains) which extract the greater part of the moisture carried by the prevailing south west and west winds. Gale force is seldom attained.

The warmth of spring and summer is usually accompanied by the low humidity - official statistics show that Ross enjoys almost the lowest atmospheric humidity in this country in the spring months. High humidity, when accompanied by a high temperature, renders the air very oppressive and enervating - so this prevalence of low humidity makes for personal comfort.

F.J. Parsons, Meteorological Officer, Ross Observatory, 1930s

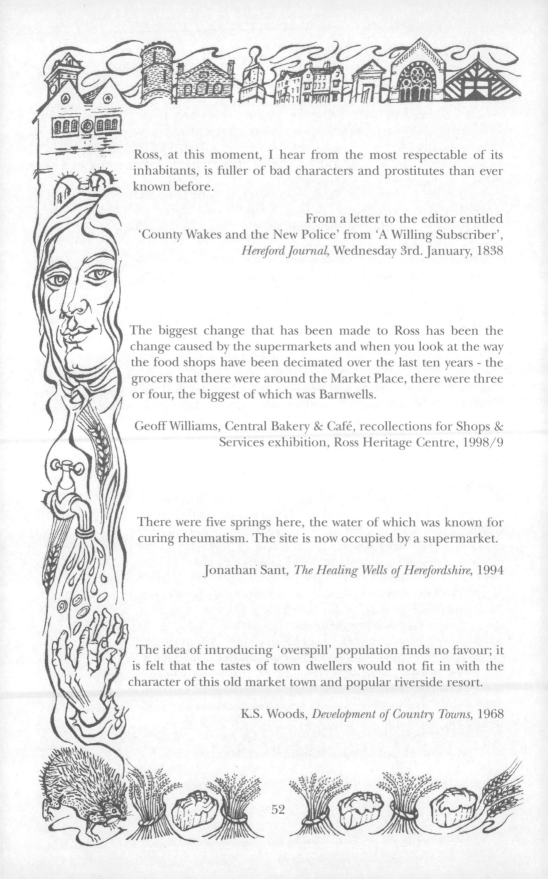

Ross, at this moment, I hear from the most respectable of its inhabitants, is fuller of bad characters and prostitutes than ever known before.

From a letter to the editor entitled 'County Wakes and the New Police' from 'A Willing Subscriber', *Hereford Journal*, Wednesday 3rd. January, 1838

The biggest change that has been made to Ross has been the change caused by the supermarkets and when you look at the way the food shops have been decimated over the last ten years - the grocers that there were around the Market Place, there were three or four, the biggest of which was Barnwells.

Geoff Williams, Central Bakery & Café, recollections for Shops & Services exhibition, Ross Heritage Centre, 1998/9

There were five springs here, the water of which was known for curing rheumatism. The site is now occupied by a supermarket.

Jonathan Sant, *The Healing Wells of Herefordshire*, 1994

The idea of introducing 'overspill' population finds no favour; it is felt that the tastes of town dwellers would not fit in with the character of this old market town and popular riverside resort.

K.S. Woods, *Development of Country Towns*, 1968

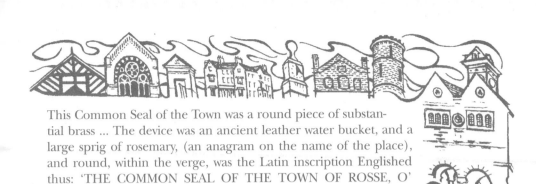

This Common Seal of the Town was a round piece of substantial brass ... The device was an ancient leather water bucket, and a large sprig of rosemary, (an anagram on the name of the place), and round, within the verge, was the Latin inscription Englished thus: 'THE COMMON SEAL OF THE TOWN OF ROSSE, O' CHRIST BLESS.'

T.B. Watkins, The Ross Guide, 1827

The Ross coat of arms has a shield divided across into red and green. In the red portion are three leopards' faces reversed with fleurs de lys thrust through, which appear in the diocesan arms and commemorate Ross being the Manor of the Bishops of Hereford. The blue and white wave represents the Wye and the green portion has a fleur de lys from the arms of John Kyrle and an emblem of the Blessed Virgin Mary. Above the shield is a closed helm surrounded by decorative mantling in green and white. The helm is surmounted by an ancient crown of fleurs de lys, representing the devolution of Ross to the Crown in 1559. From the cross rises a golden eagle, referring to the Roman association with the district. It wears a green collar and its breast and wings are charged with three red roses, an heraldic pun on the name, 'Ross'.

Martin H. Morris, The Book of Ross-on-Wye, 1980

> The hedgehog - erst in prickly ball -
> Now stands of Kyrle the crest;
> And thrice on shield of Abrahall
> The urchin's form's impressed! ...

The hedgehog signifieth a man expert in gathering of substance, and one that providently layeth hold upon proffered opportunity, and so 'making hay' as we say proverbially, 'whilst the sun doth shine,' preventeth future want.

This small animal, whose body is armed like a phalanx facing the enemy on all sides, was depicted on the shield to intimate that the bearer was ready to answer any attack from his antagonist.

J.A. Stratford, The Wye Tour, 1896

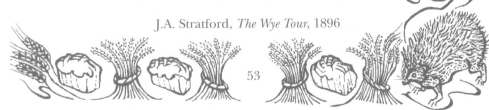

BENEFACTORS

Ross was not short of public benefactors at that period. Amongst such should be mentioned Walter Scott, son of a poor tradesman of the town, who eventually acquired a small fortune in London, came back to his native village and left £200 a year to educate 30 boys and 30 girls in the Walter Scott school. Webb, another native, founded a hospital or Alms house in Copse Cross Street for seven poor people. There were also gifts of almshouses, by Rudhall, Pye and other natives of Ross which all tend to indicate a kindness of heart which was astounding, and the poor of Ross still enjoy these ancient privileges.

Alfred Greer, *Ross, the River Wye & the Forest of Dean*, 1947

It may here be remarked that the numerous public charities in such a small town as Ross give evidence of the benevolent character of the men the town and neighbourhood have produced. There are five distinct sets of almshouses, some of them liberally endowed, viz. Webbe's, Rudhall's, and Perrock's Hospitals; Pye's and Markey's Almshouses; besides Baker's Charity, numbers of bread charities, gifts, doles, &c. ...

The Blue Coat (or Walter Scott's) School, in Old Gloucester Road, was founded by Dr. Whiting in 1709; but, after falling into partial disuse, was restored and endowed by Mr. Walter Scott, who, acquiring a large fortune by trade in London, and having no family to whom he could leave his money, bequeathed about £7,000 for the erection of a schoolhouse, and the clothing and educating of 30 boys and the same number of girls, children of the inhabitants of the town.

A curious tale is told of Mr. Walter Scott, which, if not exactly true, we may do no harm by relating. It is said of him, 'that when a boy, he had taken some pears from a garden, and, being seen eating of them by a man who guessed where they came from, the man told the boy he would be hanged if he was found out. Terrified at this threat, he instantly left Ross and made his way to London, where he set up as a plasterer, and, taken in hand by his uncle, he acquired a fortune in trade, which he spent in endowing the school wherein he had received his early education.'

J.A. Stratford, *The Wye Tour*, 1896

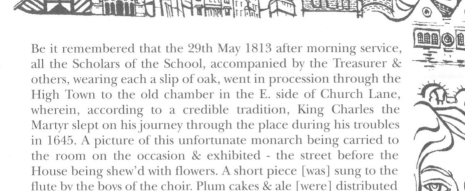

Be it remembered that the 29th May 1813 after morning service, all the Scholars of the School, accompanied by the Treasurer & others, wearing each a slip of oak, went in procession through the High Town to the old chamber in the E. side of Church Lane, wherein, according to a credible tradition, King Charles the Martyr slept on his journey through the place during his troubles in 1645. A picture of this unfortunate monarch being carried to the room on the occasion & exhibited - the street before the House being shew'd with flowers. A short piece [was] sung to the flute by the boys of the choir. Plum cakes & ale [were] distributed to all who attended.

N.B. The Chamber, of late, divided into two, is one part of an Inn, formerly called 'Gabriel Hill's Gt. Inn'. A reputed piece of the Oak Bedstead on which the King repas'd, is placed in front of the Boys Reading Desk in the School House.

Copied by Winifred Leeds from
The Walter Scott School Minute Book, 1798-1860

It would not be fitting to conclude without a word of appreciation respecting a townsman of our own days who, beginning as a charity boy receiving his education at the Walter Scott school, worked his way through obstacles and difficulties to become a most respected Magistrate and Alderman, and Member of Parliament for Leominster. He was subsequently elected by a very large majority as the first Member for the Forest of Dean. His name was Thomas Blake. His many benefactions and his love for his native town, entitle his name to be added to the list given before. His death occurred on March 31st 1901, but his name will be remembered and revered for ever.

Their spirit lit the town three hundred years ago
Illumed the darkness for a while
Then flickerd out, and died.
Who caught again that ancient flame?
relit the lamp
where Faith, and Hope and Charity abide?
Twas Thomas Blake, each man of Ross replied.

Alfred Greer, *Ross, the River Wye & the Forest of Dean*, 1947

MARKET & FARM STOCK

The market day is Thursday, for corn, butter, cheese, vegetables, &c. Every fourth Thursday is a monthly market for cattle &c. Fairs are held in the town on the first Thursday after the 10th March, for sheep, &c.; on Holy Thursday and Trinity Thursday, for fancy goods; on July 20th, for wool, &c.; first Thursday after the 10th October, for cheese; and on December 11th, for horses, sheep, &c.

Cassey's *History, Topography & Directory of Herefordshire*, 1858

James Wood was summoned at the instance of Superintendent Moore for allowing a nuisance to exist on his premises. The Superintendent stated that the nuisance arose from defendant keeping pigs in the rear of his premises; he had first of all given a verbal notice for the removal of the nuisance, and as no heed was taken, he delivered a written notice; finding the nuisance had not been abated, he served the defendant with a summons; and since then the pigs had been removed. Defendant denied that any nuisance had been created; his pigsty was situated between the road to the One Mill and the road to the Hom; and could be no nuisance, as it had existed there for centuries. The Bench: What do you mean for centuries? Defendant: Why, about three generations. The Bench: And how many years constitute a century? Defendant: (considering a moment), Why, fifty years (laughter). The defendant wished to call a witness in support of his testimony that no nuisance had been created, but on being given to understand that this would add to his expenses, he wished to know the amount already incurred. On being told that the expenses came to 6s., he appeared satisfied and agreed to let it stop at that, observing that 'it was pretty tidy' (much laughter in which the Bench joined.) The money was paid, the defendant remarking that he had taken down part of the sty, and would go home and pull down the rest.

Ross Gazette, 1860s

The Medical Officer, Dr. C.C. Cocks, reported in 1880 that 263 pigs were being kept in the town. There were 19 in High Street, four in Broad Street and no fewer than 52 in Brookend Street. Commissioners complained about the stench, but not wishing to impose undue hardship, took no decisive steps, though within a few years the keeping of pigs in the populated areas was to be prohibited.

Martin H. Morris, *The Book of Ross-on-Wye*, 1980

An occasion arose in 1854 when a number of High Church Anglicans sought to have the traditional Ross Fair prohibited on Ascension Day. This Fair, held regularly every Thursday, had been granted to the Manor of Ross by King Stephen, and it was confirmed by Henry III who added four other fairs to the weekly one, these to be held on Ascension Day, Corpus Christi Day, St. Margaret's Day and St. Andrew's Day. A meeting to decide the fate of the Fair was held at the Royal Hotel in Ross, and Lewis, as a member of the Camden Society and a man well known for his knowledge of local history, addressed the meeting on the legal aspects of the matter and the history of the Fair. Discussion afterwards was heated ... [though] finally it was voted to continue to hold the Fair on Ascension Day.

Rev. T.T. Lewis, 1854

There formerly existed a certain tenement called the Boothall, used for the purpose of holding a Court of Piepowder.

This Court (always held in fairs) was established to do justice to buyers and sellers, and for redress of disorders committed in them; so called because they were most used in summer, when the suitors in Court had dusty feet, and from the expedition in hearing cases relating thereto, before the dust went off the feet of the plaintiffs and defendants. ...

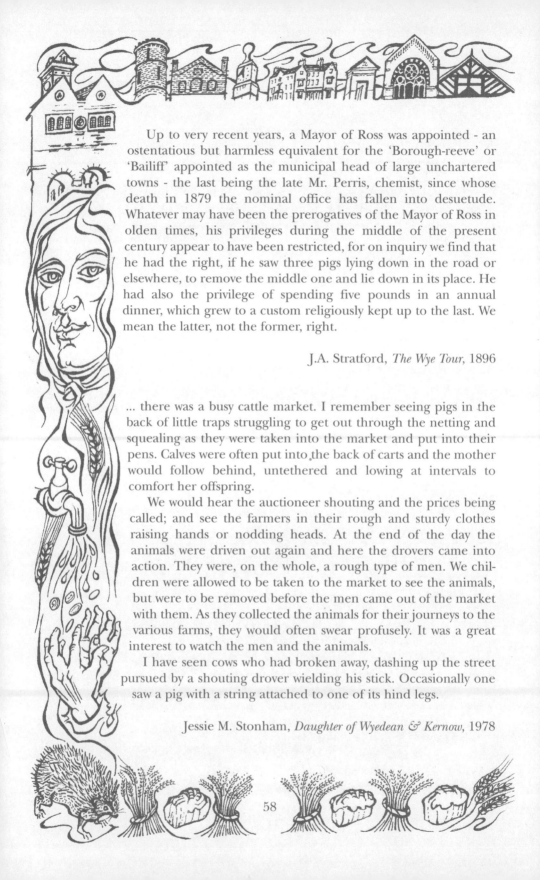

Up to very recent years, a Mayor of Ross was appointed - an ostentatious but harmless equivalent for the 'Borough-reeve' or 'Bailiff' appointed as the municipal head of large unchartered towns - the last being the late Mr. Perris, chemist, since whose death in 1879 the nominal office has fallen into desuetude. Whatever may have been the prerogatives of the Mayor of Ross in olden times, his privileges during the middle of the present century appear to have been restricted, for on inquiry we find that he had the right, if he saw three pigs lying down in the road or elsewhere, to remove the middle one and lie down in its place. He had also the privilege of spending five pounds in an annual dinner, which grew to a custom religiously kept up to the last. We mean the latter, not the former, right.

J.A. Stratford, *The Wye Tour*, 1896

... there was a busy cattle market. I remember seeing pigs in the back of little traps struggling to get out through the netting and squealing as they were taken into the market and put into their pens. Calves were often put into the back of carts and the mother would follow behind, untethered and lowing at intervals to comfort her offspring.

We would hear the auctioneer shouting and the prices being called; and see the farmers in their rough and sturdy clothes raising hands or nodding heads. At the end of the day the animals were driven out again and here the drovers came into action. They were, on the whole, a rough type of men. We children were allowed to be taken to the market to see the animals, but were to be removed before the men came out of the market with them. As they collected the animals for their journeys to the various farms, they would often swear profusely. It was a great interest to watch the men and the animals.

I have seen cows who had broken away, dashing up the street pursued by a shouting drover wielding his stick. Occasionally one saw a pig with a string attached to one of its hind legs.

Jessie M. Stonham, *Daughter of Wyedean & Kernow*, 1978

TRADE

Though not distinguished by historical occurrences, or celebrated for any important handicraft productions, Ross seems to have enjoyed, in the 16th century, a provincial reputation for its boots. Lord Talbot, writing from Goodrich Castle to his noble father in 1576, states: 'According to my ryches and the countery I dwell in, and not my desyre I send yor Lordshipp a Monmouth Cappe and a rundlett of Perry and I muste require pardon to name the other homely thynge, a payre of Rosse Bootes, which yi they be fytt for yor Ldship, you may have as many as pleas you to appoynt.'

Lord Talbot, 1576

Ross was at one time much noted for its iron works, but at present there is no manufactory carried on in an extensive way. The mechanic trades common to all towns are exercised here, and the shops are well supplied with every necessary article for the use of the Town and Neighbourhood.

T.B. Watkins, *The Ross Guide*, 1827

Trade directories ... list a magnificent range of professions and skills, every conceivable thing from artists to auctioneers, bakers, bankers, basket makers and blacksmiths, including one woman smithy, Mary Ann Palmer. There were boat owners, booksellers, boot and shoe repairers (nearly two dozen of these), brewers, butchers, cabinet makers, carpenters, cheese and bacon factors, coal dealers, chemists, corn factors, coach makers, fancy goods repositories, coopers, china and glass dealers, salt sellers and sauce manufacturers, sack contractors, sculptors, seed merchants, stockbrokers, toy dealers, tanners and tallow chandlers, even a straw bonnet warehouse, hatters, glovers, fishing tackle dealers, leather sellers and one Daniel O'Connell who made elastic stockings, wristlets and kneecaps.

Jon Hurley, *Thomas Blake, Pious Benefactor*

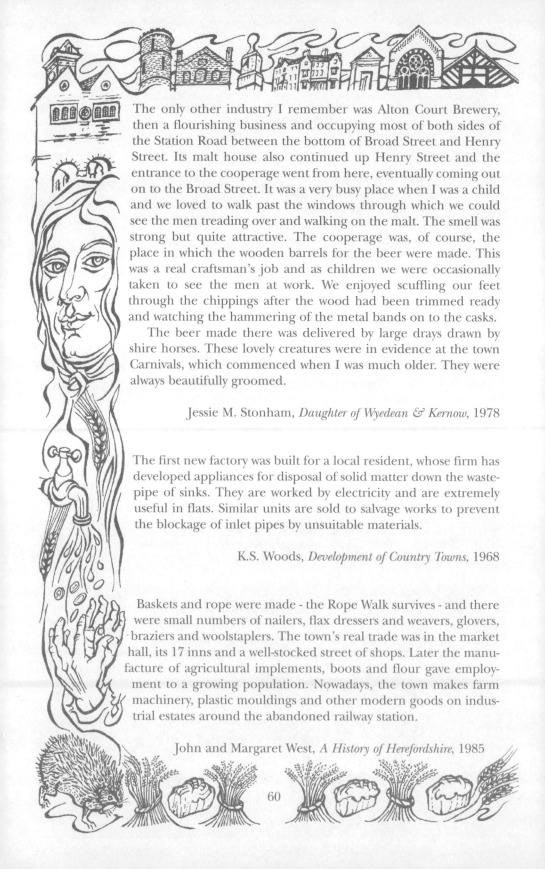

The only other industry I remember was Alton Court Brewery, then a flourishing business and occupying most of both sides of the Station Road between the bottom of Broad Street and Henry Street. Its malt house also continued up Henry Street and the entrance to the cooperage went from here, eventually coming out on to the Broad Street. It was a very busy place when I was a child and we loved to walk past the windows through which we could see the men treading over and walking on the malt. The smell was strong but quite attractive. The cooperage was, of course, the place in which the wooden barrels for the beer were made. This was a real craftsman's job and as children we were occasionally taken to see the men at work. We enjoyed scuffling our feet through the chippings after the wood had been trimmed ready and watching the hammering of the metal bands on to the casks.

The beer made there was delivered by large drays drawn by shire horses. These lovely creatures were in evidence at the town Carnivals, which commenced when I was much older. They were always beautifully groomed.

Jessie M. Stonham, *Daughter of Wyedean & Kernow*, 1978

The first new factory was built for a local resident, whose firm has developed appliances for disposal of solid matter down the waste-pipe of sinks. They are worked by electricity and are extremely useful in flats. Similar units are sold to salvage works to prevent the blockage of inlet pipes by unsuitable materials.

K.S. Woods, *Development of Country Towns*, 1968

Baskets and rope were made - the Rope Walk survives - and there were small numbers of nailers, flax dressers and weavers, glovers, braziers and woolstaplers. The town's real trade was in the market hall, its 17 inns and a well-stocked street of shops. Later the manufacture of agricultural implements, boots and flour gave employment to a growing population. Nowadays, the town makes farm machinery, plastic mouldings and other modern goods on industrial estates around the abandoned railway station.

John and Margaret West, *A History of Herefordshire*, 1985

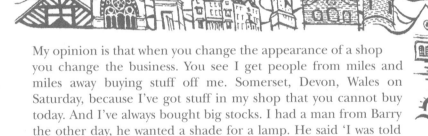

My opinion is that when you change the appearance of a shop you change the business. You see I get people from miles and miles away buying stuff off me. Somerset, Devon, Wales on Saturday, because I've got stuff in my shop that you cannot buy today. And I've always bought big stocks. I had a man from Barry the other day, he wanted a shade for a lamp. He said 'I was told you had got them.'

A friend of mine rang me up one day. 'What have you been up to?' he said. 'Nothing particular,' I said. 'Why, what's the matter?' 'Well, my wife picked up a magazine, it's called the *Living Period*. It's a special furniture book, one of the best books in England. And in there somebody had wrote about getting wicks and mantles and one thing and another and they were told the only place they would be able to get it would be 'George Nicholls in Ross-on-Wye.' I don't know who put it in and it finished off, 'if he hasn't got it, you can give up.'

George Nicholls, Seventy Four Years in Hardware, 1998

FIRE

The town's only fire-fighting appliances were wooden tanks on wheels, that had been kept in the north porch of the parish church since 1809. On Thursday 15th April, 1852, a large number of men fought unsuccessfully to prevent fire destroying 30 acres of Chase Wood and early next morning the need for a proper fire engine became even more desperate.

Fire engulfed the premises in New Street of the Ross and Forest of Dean Bank and the offices of Hall and Minett. Henry Minett, his wife and six children, governess and cook, were all brought by ladders to safety, but a 17-year-old maid servant, Emma Bird, died.

Hundreds of men and women formed lines up and down the street, bringing water from house pumps and rain butts, and hogsheads were brought by horse and trap. Still the fire raged. The brigade from Llandinabo took an hour to arrive and that from Hereford two hours. The Ross appliances were useless.

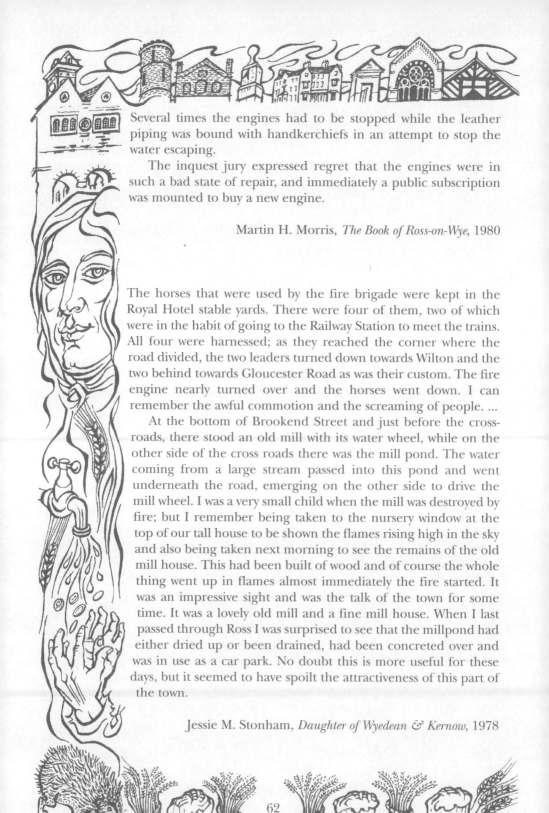

Several times the engines had to be stopped while the leather piping was bound with handkerchiefs in an attempt to stop the water escaping.

The inquest jury expressed regret that the engines were in such a bad state of repair, and immediately a public subscription was mounted to buy a new engine.

Martin H. Morris, *The Book of Ross-on-Wye*, 1980

The horses that were used by the fire brigade were kept in the Royal Hotel stable yards. There were four of them, two of which were in the habit of going to the Railway Station to meet the trains. All four were harnessed; as they reached the corner where the road divided, the two leaders turned down towards Wilton and the two behind towards Gloucester Road as was their custom. The fire engine nearly turned over and the horses went down. I can remember the awful commotion and the screaming of people. ...

At the bottom of Brookend Street and just before the cross-roads, there stood an old mill with its water wheel, while on the other side of the cross roads there was the mill pond. The water coming from a large stream passed into this pond and went underneath the road, emerging on the other side to drive the mill wheel. I was a very small child when the mill was destroyed by fire; but I remember being taken to the nursery window at the top of our tall house to be shown the flames rising high in the sky and also being taken next morning to see the remains of the old mill house. This had been built of wood and of course the whole thing went up in flames almost immediately the fire started. It was an impressive sight and was the talk of the town for some time. It was a lovely old mill and a fine mill house. When I last passed through Ross I was surprised to see that the millpond had either dried up or been drained, had been concreted over and was in use as a car park. No doubt this is more useful for these days, but it seemed to have spoilt the attractiveness of this part of the town.

Jessie M. Stonham, *Daughter of Wyedean & Kernow*, 1978

BED & BOARD

At 5 oClock we dined & were not very pleased with our entertainment. The fowls were tough, and the wine very bad.

At Ross our dinners were charged 2s.6d. each - Wine 4s.6d. a bottle - Brandy 6s. a bottle. Breakfasts 1s. 3d. - Beds 1s. each. The Landlord never made his appearance to us, and on the whole we were glad to shift our quarters.

Joseph Farrington's *Diaries*, 1803

There is no professed Lodging House in Ross, but Lodgings may be taken at many private houses, kept by persons in business, who have apartments to let for a limited time.

T.B. Watkins, *The Ross Guide*, 1827

It is, however, certain that the influx of visitors to our pretty Town has steadily increased from the date of the completion of its commodious and finely placed [Royal] Hotel. The salubrity of the site is undeniable, and not long ago a septuagenarian, in gratitude for the benefit his health had derived, alike from the air and the excellent cuisine, insisted upon having this quaint motto painted in large type outside the Hotel, ICI ON RAJEUNIT. (Here you grow young again), a waggishly intended jingle, perhaps upon the familiar announcement at French restaurants, 'Déjeuners à la fourchette.'

G. Strong, *Handbook to Ross and Archenfield*, 1863

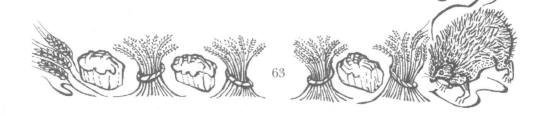

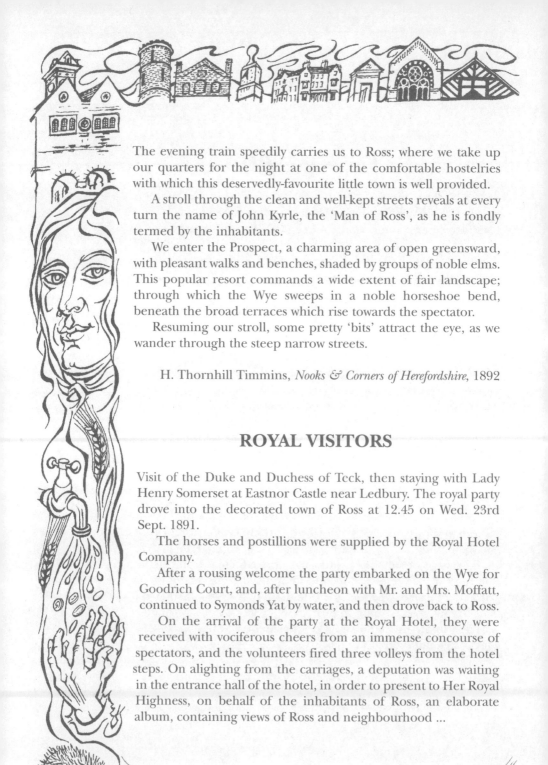

The evening train speedily carries us to Ross; where we take up our quarters for the night at one of the comfortable hostelries with which this deservedly-favourite little town is well provided.

A stroll through the clean and well-kept streets reveals at every turn the name of John Kyrle, the 'Man of Ross', as he is fondly termed by the inhabitants.

We enter the Prospect, a charming area of open greensward, with pleasant walks and benches, shaded by groups of noble elms. This popular resort commands a wide extent of fair landscape; through which the Wye sweeps in a noble horseshoe bend, beneath the broad terraces which rise towards the spectator.

Resuming our stroll, some pretty 'bits' attract the eye, as we wander through the steep narrow streets.

H. Thornhill Timmins, *Nooks & Corners of Herefordshire*, 1892

ROYAL VISITORS

Visit of the Duke and Duchess of Teck, then staying with Lady Henry Somerset at Eastnor Castle near Ledbury. The royal party drove into the decorated town of Ross at 12.45 on Wed. 23rd Sept. 1891.

The horses and postillions were supplied by the Royal Hotel Company.

After a rousing welcome the party embarked on the Wye for Goodrich Court, and, after luncheon with Mr. and Mrs. Moffatt, continued to Symonds Yat by water, and then drove back to Ross.

On the arrival of the party at the Royal Hotel, they were received with vociferous cheers from an immense concourse of spectators, and the volunteers fired three volleys from the hotel steps. On alighting from the carriages, a deputation was waiting in the entrance hall of the hotel, in order to present to Her Royal Highness, on behalf of the inhabitants of Ross, an elaborate album, containing views of Ross and neighbourhood ...

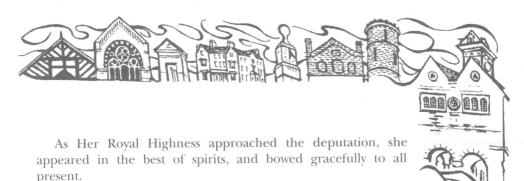

As Her Royal Highness approached the deputation, she appeared in the best of spirits, and bowed gracefully to all present.

... The Royal party left amidst the heartiest cheering, being again escorted by the Yeomanry, Volunteers, and Fire Brigade with lighted torches; the band playing 'The Girl I Left Behind Me.' The procession was followed to the outskirts of the town by a big crowd.

Ross Gazette, 1891

The late Mr. T. W. Purchas, of Ross, gave the following account:- The visit of King George the Fourth to Ross, in the year 1821, appears to have been an unexpected one, and was caused by the ship in which he crossed from Ireland having been driven out of her course by bad weather, landing him in South Wales, instead of at Holyhead or Liverpool. He entered the town by the old Wilton road and Dock Pitch (then the only way), and after a change of horses, and taking a glass of wine that was handed to him by Mrs. Mary Howells, the landlady of the King's Head, much to the disappointment of the inhabitants, he drew down the blinds of the coach, intending to hurry on as quickly as possible. Greatly to his disgust, however, on arriving at the Nag's Head, an unexpected obstacle barred his progress for a time. The carrier's waggon had arrived, and, before unloading, the horses had been taken out. The place was so narrow that the King was obliged to wait while the horses were brought out again, and the waggon moved out of his way. This incident led to a great improvement of the town, as, shortly afterwards, notice was sent from London that, unless a better way was made through the town, the mail would be taken off the road, in consequence of which the present Gloucester road was constructed.

Edward Foord, *Cathedrals, Abbeys & Famous Churches*, 1925

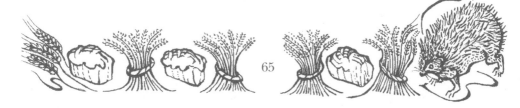

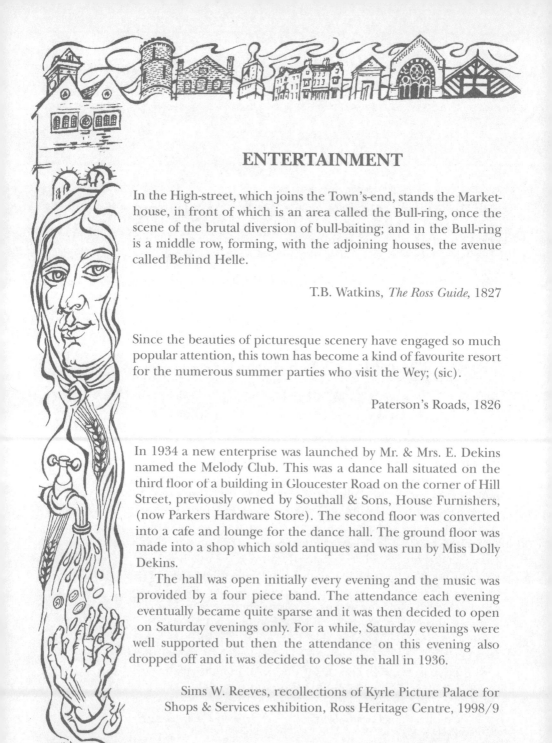

ENTERTAINMENT

In the High-street, which joins the Town's-end, stands the Market-house, in front of which is an area called the Bull-ring, once the scene of the brutal diversion of bull-baiting; and in the Bull-ring is a middle row, forming, with the adjoining houses, the avenue called Behind Helle.

T.B. Watkins, *The Ross Guide*, 1827

Since the beauties of picturesque scenery have engaged so much popular attention, this town has become a kind of favourite resort for the numerous summer parties who visit the Wey; (sic).

Paterson's Roads, 1826

In 1934 a new enterprise was launched by Mr. & Mrs. E. Dekins named the Melody Club. This was a dance hall situated on the third floor of a building in Gloucester Road on the corner of Hill Street, previously owned by Southall & Sons, House Furnishers, (now Parkers Hardware Store). The second floor was converted into a cafe and lounge for the dance hall. The ground floor was made into a shop which sold antiques and was run by Miss Dolly Dekins.

The hall was open initially every evening and the music was provided by a four piece band. The attendance each evening eventually became quite sparse and it was then decided to open on Saturday evenings only. For a while, Saturday evenings were well supported but then the attendance on this evening also dropped off and it was decided to close the hall in 1936.

Sims W. Reeves, recollections of Kyrle Picture Palace for Shops & Services exhibition, Ross Heritage Centre, 1998/9

The boys played marbles, which were of many colours. The game was usually played on the playground or travelling along the edge of the road, something that would be out of the question in this age of many and speedy motor cars. Coloured 'allys', as the superior kind of marbles were named, were also collected and treasured. The girls, too, had their hoops, but they were of wood and were driven with a stick. Skipping ropes were very popular and longer ones were used in the playground for more communal games.

Jessie M. Stonham, *Daughter of Wyedean & Kernow*, 1978

During the First World War, 1914 to 1918, news reels of the war were shown and also silent films. Some of these were in serial form, i.e. episodes each week, usually ending at a critical or exciting point, thereby encouraging people to come to the Cinema the next week to see what happened! Some of the people became very worked up by these films and actually believed that they were taking part in the various scenes. I witnessed on a number of occasions people shouting 'look out, he is behind you and he has a knife or a gun in his hand', or 'don't go into that room or elsewhere, he or they are waiting for you.' The person often performed the actions taking place in the film. Suitable music to suit and enhance the scenes was played by the pianist, in this case Miss A. Dallimore, daughter of Mr. Dallimore, Footwear Retailer, Gloucester Road. She was later replaced by Mr. J. Harrison, Piano and Mrs. Jerrod, Violin, in 1927. ...

A local character nicknamed 'Tally' used to sit in an ancient bathchair in the gutter outside the cinema playing a scratchy old gramaphone. Many people entering the cinema felt sorry for him and dropped a coin or coins in his tin. In addition, a middle aged couple, Mr. & Mrs. Baker, who pushed a mobile organ (Irdy Girdy) around the streets of Ross, would sometimes stop and give a musical interlude. This was accomplished by turning a handle attached to the organ which must have made their arms very tired. ...

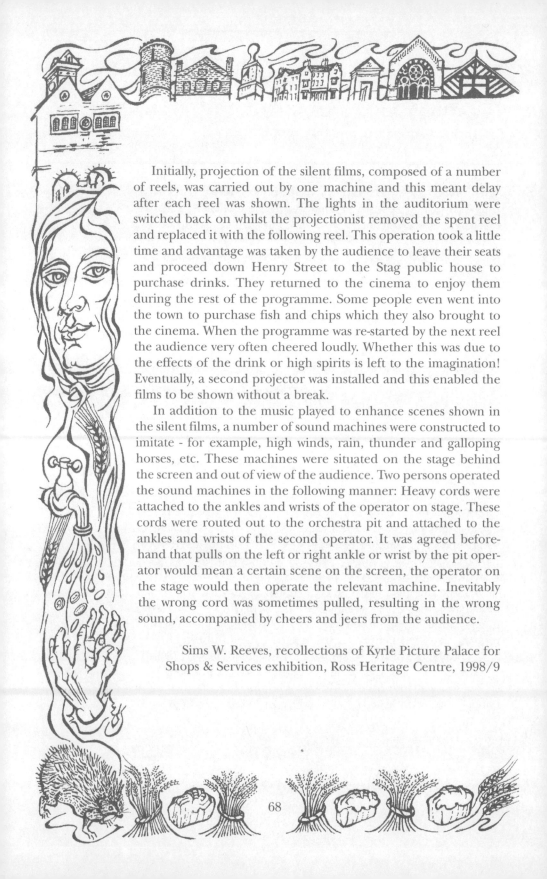

Initially, projection of the silent films, composed of a number of reels, was carried out by one machine and this meant delay after each reel was shown. The lights in the auditorium were switched back on whilst the projectionist removed the spent reel and replaced it with the following reel. This operation took a little time and advantage was taken by the audience to leave their seats and proceed down Henry Street to the Stag public house to purchase drinks. They returned to the cinema to enjoy them during the rest of the programme. Some people even went into the town to purchase fish and chips which they also brought to the cinema. When the programme was re-started by the next reel the audience very often cheered loudly. Whether this was due to the effects of the drink or high spirits is left to the imagination! Eventually, a second projector was installed and this enabled the films to be shown without a break.

In addition to the music played to enhance scenes shown in the silent films, a number of sound machines were constructed to imitate - for example, high winds, rain, thunder and galloping horses, etc. These machines were situated on the stage behind the screen and out of view of the audience. Two persons operated the sound machines in the following manner: Heavy cords were attached to the ankles and wrists of the operator on stage. These cords were routed out to the orchestra pit and attached to the ankles and wrists of the second operator. It was agreed before-hand that pulls on the left or right ankle or wrist by the pit operator would mean a certain scene on the screen, the operator on the stage would then operate the relevant machine. Inevitably the wrong cord was sometimes pulled, resulting in the wrong sound, accompanied by cheers and jeers from the audience.

Sims W. Reeves, recollections of Kyrle Picture Palace for Shops & Services exhibition, Ross Heritage Centre, 1998/9

IN POETRY

Will Ross' bold Prospect charm the eye,
Kissing with tapering spire the sky, -
And tell how Kyrle, of God-like mind,
(Meek benefactor of mankind)
With generous hand relieved the poor,
Who o'er found welcome at his door,
Promoting virtue, love, and truth,
Rich crowns of age, best guides of youth!
Nor pass we Wilton's crumbling towers,
O'erspread with ivy and wild flowers.

From 'The Banks of the Wye' by James Henry James, 1856

Nor distant far, Ross, with her wood-clad hills,
O'er meads and corn-fields thick, complacent smiles;
A landscape painting to the mind and eye,
Such only found where flows the matchless Wye.
Now quits the Muse her pleasing task to guide,
But bids the thoughtful rambler turn aside.

From 'Herefordia' by James Henry James, 1861

Most noble Lord, the pillar of my life,
And patron of my Muse's pupilage,
Thro' whose large bounty poured on me rife,
In the first season of my feeble age,
I now do live, bound yours by vassalage.

From a sonnet to Lord Grey of Wilton Castle from
Edmund Spenser who, under the Ross nobleman's patronage,
wrote his 'Faery Queen'

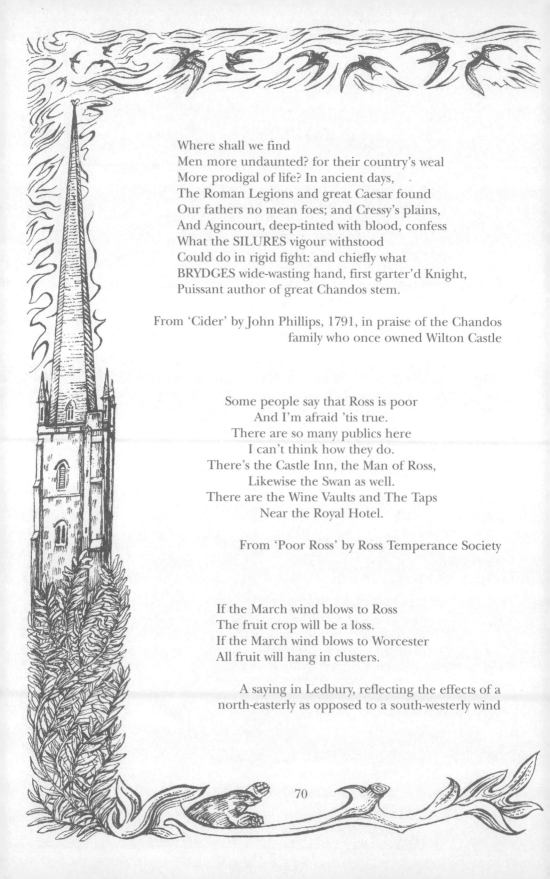

Where shall we find
Men more undaunted? for their country's weal
More prodigal of life? In ancient days,
The Roman Legions and great Caesar found
Our fathers no mean foes; and Cressy's plains,
And Agincourt, deep-tinted with blood, confess
What the SILURES vigour withstood
Could do in rigid fight: and chiefly what
BRYDGES wide-wasting hand, first garter'd Knight,
Puissant author of great Chandos stem.

From 'Cider' by John Phillips, 1791, in praise of the Chandos
family who once owned Wilton Castle

Some people say that Ross is poor
And I'm afraid 'tis true.
There are so many publics here
I can't think how they do.
There's the Castle Inn, the Man of Ross,
Likewise the Swan as well.
There are the Wine Vaults and The Taps
Near the Royal Hotel.

From 'Poor Ross' by Ross Temperance Society

If the March wind blows to Ross
The fruit crop will be a loss.
If the March wind blows to Worcester
All fruit will hang in clusters.

A saying in Ledbury, reflecting the effects of a
north-easterly as opposed to a south-westerly wind

TRANSPORT

In the course of years, Ariconium or Rose town (so called from the red sandstone rocks or from the red colour of its soil) became quite a busy and prosperous colony, with trackways radiating from it in all directions. Many of these early British trackways may still be trod here and there, although some 2000 years have elapsed since they were first made.

Alfred Greer, *Ross, the River Wye & the Forest of Dean*, 1947

The clay loam which prevails throughout Herefordshire, a moist climate, and the constant alternation of hill and dale, are, of course, unfavourable alike to the construction and maintenance of good roads. Oxen had often to be employed in order to drag hapless coaches out of the deep ruts with which the highways abounded, and there is something suggestive in the repeated injunctions given by Sergeant Hoskyns in writing to his house-keeper, 'to provide a good coach with four horses to meet him at Ross (only a few miles from his home) and above all to study the coach-way; where to break hedges, and how to avoid deep and dangerous ways.' Even at the commencement of the present century a writer says that the roads were such as one might expect to meet with in the marshes of Holland, or among the mountains of Switzerland; and it was gravely debated, not many years ago, whether it would not cost as little to make the highway between Kington and Leominster navigable as to to make it hard!

J.A. Stratford, *The Wye Tour*, 1896

The present Commissioners of the turnpike trust have converted to a general benefit, - by taking down the Causeway, and raising the whole breadth of road out of the reach of these temporary evils; so that it now presents, from the end of Wilton Bridge, to which it adjoins, a 'spacious driving way', and is a fine termination of the beautiful approach to Ross either from Monmouth or from Hereford.

Charles Heath, *Excursion Down the Wye from Ross to Monmouth*, 1799

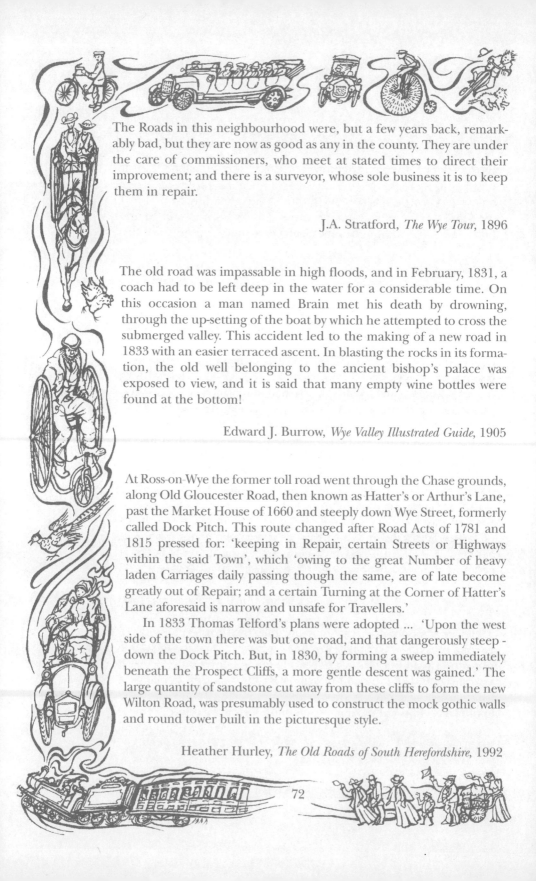

The Roads in this neighbourhood were, but a few years back, remarkably bad, but they are now as good as any in the county. They are under the care of commissioners, who meet at stated times to direct their improvement; and there is a surveyor, whose sole business it is to keep them in repair.

J.A. Stratford, *The Wye Tour*, 1896

The old road was impassable in high floods, and in February, 1831, a coach had to be left deep in the water for a considerable time. On this occasion a man named Brain met his death by drowning, through the up-setting of the boat by which he attempted to cross the submerged valley. This accident led to the making of a new road in 1833 with an easier terraced ascent. In blasting the rocks in its formation, the old well belonging to the ancient bishop's palace was exposed to view, and it is said that many empty wine bottles were found at the bottom!

Edward J. Burrow, *Wye Valley Illustrated Guide*, 1905

At Ross-on-Wye the former toll road went through the Chase grounds, along Old Gloucester Road, then known as Hatter's or Arthur's Lane, past the Market House of 1660 and steeply down Wye Street, formerly called Dock Pitch. This route changed after Road Acts of 1781 and 1815 pressed for: 'keeping in Repair, certain Streets or Highways within the said Town', which 'owing to the great Number of heavy laden Carriages daily passing though the same, are of late become greatly out of Repair; and a certain Turning at the Corner of Hatter's Lane aforesaid is narrow and unsafe for Travellers.'

In 1833 Thomas Telford's plans were adopted ... 'Upon the west side of the town there was but one road, and that dangerously steep - down the Dock Pitch. But, in 1830, by forming a sweep immediately beneath the Prospect Cliffs, a more gentle descent was gained.' The large quantity of sandstone cut away from these cliffs to form the new Wilton Road, was presumably used to construct the mock gothic walls and round tower built in the picturesque style.

Heather Hurley, *The Old Roads of South Herefordshire*, 1992

Ross achieved a major position on the country's coaching routes, being about 18 hours from London. No fewer than 16 coaches were passing through the town on most days in the early 19th century. Every morning except Sunday, the 'Rapid' called at 5.45 on its way from Hereford to London, and in the afternoons four coaches left for the capital; the Royal Mail from Milford, the 'Champion' from Hereford, the 'Paul Pry' from Brecon and the 'Nimrod' from Carmarthen. Coaches were also providing a service in the opposite direction, and in addition, the 'Rising Sun' called on its way from Hereford to Gloucester and the 'Man of Ross' left at 8 a.m. on Wednesday and Friday for Ledbury and Worcester.

Martin H. Morris, *The Book of Ross-on-Wye*, 1980

The London Mail, and other coaches, pass through it daily, being the high road to all parts of North and South Wales, and Ireland, which adds much to its cheerfulness at all seasons of the year....

Besides the opportunity of having Post-Chaises, persons may be accommodated by Stage Coaches, to travel in almost every direction.

The Public are also accommodated by Stage Waggons, for carrying heavy goods to and from every part of the kingdom.

T.B. Watkins, *The Ross Guide*, 1827

I can remember so many of the beautiful little ponies that were used in traps and 'tubs'. There was a lady who used to drive around Ross in a basket carriage to do her shopping. In those days the shopkeeper, or one of his assistants, would come out to anyone driving a carriage, to save them having to alight and go into the shop to buy what they needed. Small 'tubs' with a pony between the shafts were used to take children out for their morning 'airing' or to school. I remember seeing a photograph of Princess Mary driving with her two small sons in a similar 'pony and tub'.

At the time when we children had the 'tub' to drive us in to school, big timber waggons would go to Ross railway station, taking their huge tree trunks for loading on to the trucks in the sidings. On one occasion my mother was driving Kitty along the

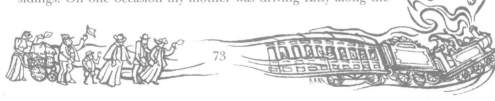

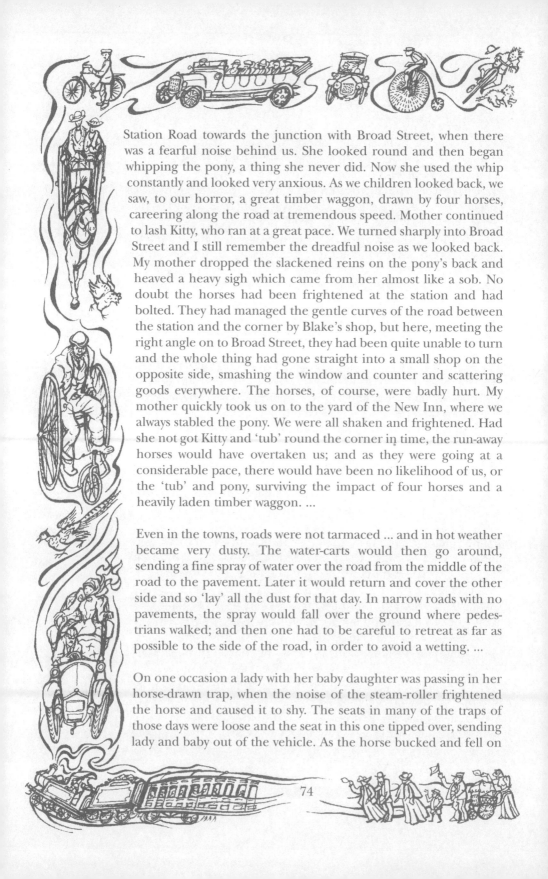

Station Road towards the junction with Broad Street, when there was a fearful noise behind us. She looked round and then began whipping the pony, a thing she never did. Now she used the whip constantly and looked very anxious. As we children looked back, we saw, to our horror, a great timber waggon, drawn by four horses, careering along the road at tremendous speed. Mother continued to lash Kitty, who ran at a great pace. We turned sharply into Broad Street and I still remember the dreadful noise as we looked back. My mother dropped the slackened reins on the pony's back and heaved a heavy sigh which came from her almost like a sob. No doubt the horses had been frightened at the station and had bolted. They had managed the gentle curves of the road between the station and the corner by Blake's shop, but here, meeting the right angle on to Broad Street, they had been quite unable to turn and the whole thing had gone straight into a small shop on the opposite side, smashing the window and counter and scattering goods everywhere. The horses, of course, were badly hurt. My mother quickly took us on to the yard of the New Inn, where we always stabled the pony. We were all shaken and frightened. Had she not got Kitty and 'tub' round the corner in time, the run-away horses would have overtaken us; and as they were going at a considerable pace, there would have been no likelihood of us, or the 'tub' and pony, surviving the impact of four horses and a heavily laden timber waggon. ...

Even in the towns, roads were not tarmaced ... and in hot weather became very dusty. The water-carts would then go around, sending a fine spray of water over the road from the middle of the road to the pavement. Later it would return and cover the other side and so 'lay' all the dust for that day. In narrow roads with no pavements, the spray would fall over the ground where pedestrians walked; and then one had to be careful to retreat as far as possible to the side of the road, in order to avoid a wetting. ...

On one occasion a lady with her baby daughter was passing in her horse-drawn trap, when the noise of the steam-roller frightened the horse and caused it to shy. The seats in many of the traps of those days were loose and the seat in this one tipped over, sending lady and baby out of the vehicle. As the horse bucked and fell on

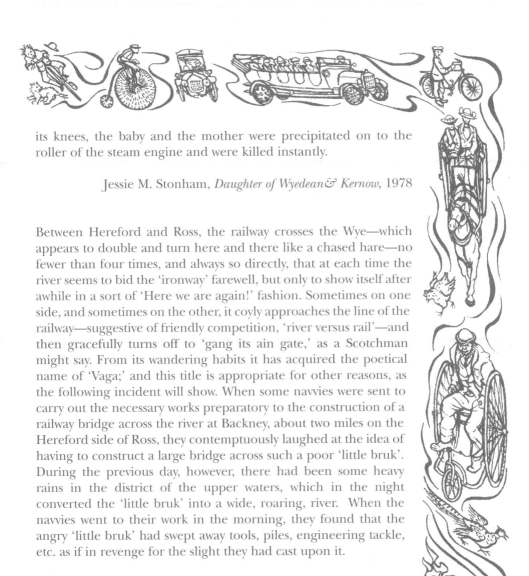

its knees, the baby and the mother were precipitated on to the roller of the steam engine and were killed instantly.

Jessie M. Stonham, *Daughter of Wyedean & Kernow*, 1978

Between Hereford and Ross, the railway crosses the Wye—which appears to double and turn here and there like a chased hare—no fewer than four times, and always so directly, that at each time the river seems to bid the 'ironway' farewell, but only to show itself after awhile in a sort of 'Here we are again!' fashion. Sometimes on one side, and sometimes on the other, it coyly approaches the line of the railway—suggestive of friendly competition, 'river versus rail'—and then gracefully turns off to 'gang its ain gate,' as a Scotchman might say. From its wandering habits it has acquired the poetical name of 'Vaga;' and this title is appropriate for other reasons, as the following incident will show. When some navvies were sent to carry out the necessary works preparatory to the construction of a railway bridge across the river at Backney, about two miles on the Hereford side of Ross, they contemptuously laughed at the idea of having to construct a large bridge across such a poor 'little bruk'. During the previous day, however, there had been some heavy rains in the district of the upper waters, which in the night converted the 'little bruk' into a wide, roaring, river. When the navvies went to their work in the morning, they found that the angry 'little bruk' had swept away tools, piles, engineering tackle, etc. as if in revenge for the slight they had cast upon it.

J.A. Stratford, *The Wye Tour*, 1896

On August 1st, 1873, Colonel Rich - the Chief Engineer of the G.W.R. - came to inspect the line. The inspecting party walked along the line, through tunnels, over bridges, peering and prodding everything they saw.

Large posters and timetables appeared all around the place and the preparations were made. But - later that night, Colonel Rich said that the line could not open as planned! He had discovered that there was no turn-table at Monmouth so the light

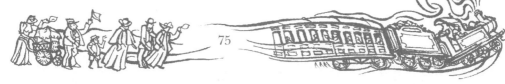

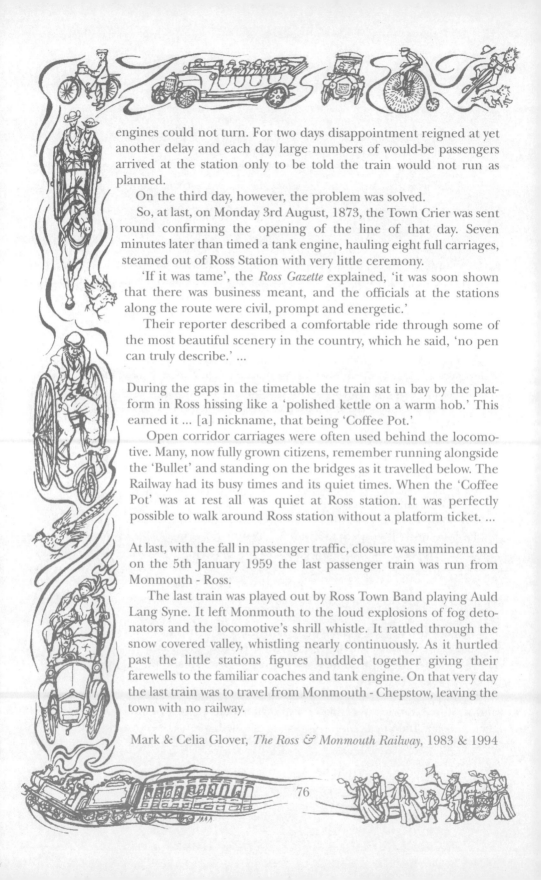

engines could not turn. For two days disappointment reigned at yet another delay and each day large numbers of would-be passengers arrived at the station only to be told the train would not run as planned.

On the third day, however, the problem was solved.

So, at last, on Monday 3rd August, 1873, the Town Crier was sent round confirming the opening of the line of that day. Seven minutes later than timed a tank engine, hauling eight full carriages, steamed out of Ross Station with very little ceremony.

'If it was tame', the *Ross Gazette* explained, 'it was soon shown that there was business meant, and the officials at the stations along the route were civil, prompt and energetic.'

Their reporter described a comfortable ride through some of the most beautiful scenery in the country, which he said, 'no pen can truly describe.' ...

During the gaps in the timetable the train sat in bay by the platform in Ross hissing like a 'polished kettle on a warm hob.' This earned it ... [a] nickname, that being 'Coffee Pot.'

Open corridor carriages were often used behind the locomotive. Many, now fully grown citizens, remember running alongside the 'Bullet' and standing on the bridges as it travelled below. The Railway had its busy times and its quiet times. When the 'Coffee Pot' was at rest all was quiet at Ross station. It was perfectly possible to walk around Ross station without a platform ticket. ...

At last, with the fall in passenger traffic, closure was imminent and on the 5th January 1959 the last passenger train was run from Monmouth - Ross.

The last train was played out by Ross Town Band playing Auld Lang Syne. It left Monmouth to the loud explosions of fog detonators and the locomotive's shrill whistle. It rattled through the snow covered valley, whistling nearly continuously. As it hurtled past the little stations figures huddled together giving their farewells to the familiar coaches and tank engine. On that very day the last train was to travel from Monmouth - Chepstow, leaving the town with no railway.

Mark & Celia Glover, *The Ross & Monmouth Railway*, 1983 & 1994

RIVER WYE

But Wye (from her dear Lug whom nothing can restrain,
In many a pleasant shade, her joy to entertain)
To Rosse her course directs; and right her name to show,
Oft windeth in her way, as back she meant to go.
Meander, who is said so intricate to be,
Hath not so many turns, nor crankling nooks as she.

Michael Drayton, from the Seventh Song in 'Poly-Olbion', 1622

The extraordinary Flood continued to rife till Wednefday morning; and, at fix o'clock (the period of its greateft height) the River Wye was two feet five inches higher than was ever known in this neighbourhood, by the oldeft inhabitant living.

The poor inhabitants of the houfes fituated beyond Wye bridge, fuffered moft feverely - they were obliged to take refuge in the upper apartments of their habitations, where they were generoufly fupplied with provifions by fome humane characters, or were brought off in boats, to prevent their finking under the accumulated miferies of hunger and cold. And here we are happy to add, that a liberal fubfcription has already been entered into, for the relief of thefe poor fufferers; notwithftanding a generous and large fubfcription which lately took place in aid of the indigent inhabitants of the city in general.

The cellars and cider-vaults fituated on both fides of the River were completely filled with water; and unfortunately a vaft quantity of cider and perry was loft, from the veffels not being properly ftopped up before they were fet afloat.

Hereford Journal, 1795 Note: This date is etched in Wilton Bridge

In the River Wye small, shrimp pink children were bathing, and in every dark patch of willows stood cows chewing the cud and letting the water ripple past their legs.

H.V. Morton, *In Search of England*, 1927

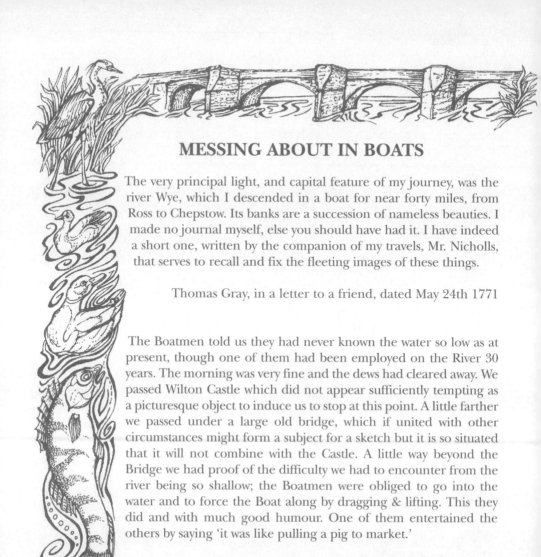

MESSING ABOUT IN BOATS

The very principal light, and capital feature of my journey, was the river Wye, which I descended in a boat for near forty miles, from Ross to Chepstow. Its banks are a succession of nameless beauties. I made no journal myself, else you should have had it. I have indeed a short one, written by the companion of my travels, Mr. Nicholls, that serves to recall and fix the fleeting images of these things.

Thomas Gray, in a letter to a friend, dated May 24th 1771

The Boatmen told us they had never known the water so low as at present, though one of them had been employed on the River 30 years. The morning was very fine and the dews had cleared away. We passed Wilton Castle which did not appear sufficiently tempting as a picturesque object to induce us to stop at this point. A little farther we passed under a large old bridge, which if united with other circumstances might form a subject for a sketch but it is so situated that it will not combine with the Castle. A little way beyond the Bridge we had proof of the difficulty we had to encounter from the river being so shallow; the Boatmen were obliged to go into the water and to force the Boat along by dragging & lifting. This they did and with much good humour. One of them entertained the others by saying 'it was like pulling a pig to market.'

Joseph Farrington's *Diaries*, 14th September, 1803

I entered a boat at Ross, on my way to Monmouth. My 'light bark' was not much unlike a gondola, when its tarpaulin cover was spread over the framework; but being favoured by a radiantly bright morning, I preferred sitting under the skeleton, and enjoying the charming scenes around me. A table in the centre of the part allotted to passengers, and cushioned seats around, made this small floating parlour a most commodious conveyance.

Thomas Roscoe, *Wanderings & Excursions*, 1837

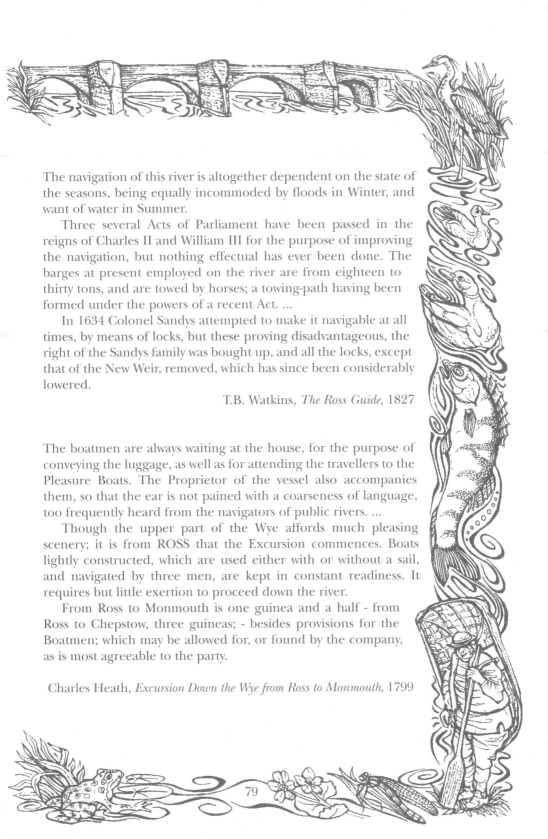

The navigation of this river is altogether dependent on the state of the seasons, being equally incommoded by floods in Winter, and want of water in Summer.

Three several Acts of Parliament have been passed in the reigns of Charles II and William III for the purpose of improving the navigation, but nothing effectual has ever been done. The barges at present employed on the river are from eighteen to thirty tons, and are towed by horses; a towing-path having been formed under the powers of a recent Act. ...

In 1634 Colonel Sandys attempted to make it navigable at all times, by means of locks, but these proving disadvantageous, the right of the Sandys family was bought up, and all the locks, except that of the New Weir, removed, which has since been considerably lowered.

T.B. Watkins, *The Ross Guide*, 1827

The boatmen are always waiting at the house, for the purpose of conveying the luggage, as well as for attending the travellers to the Pleasure Boats. The Proprietor of the vessel also accompanies them, so that the ear is not pained with a coarseness of language, too frequently heard from the navigators of public rivers. ...

Though the upper part of the Wye affords much pleasing scenery; it is from ROSS that the Excursion commences. Boats lightly constructed, which are used either with or without a sail, and navigated by three men, are kept in constant readiness. It requires but little exertion to proceed down the river.

From Ross to Monmouth is one guinea and a half - from Ross to Chepstow, three guineas; - besides provisions for the Boatmen; which may be allowed for, or found by the company, as is most agreeable to the party.

Charles Heath, *Excursion Down the Wye from Ross to Monmouth*, 1799

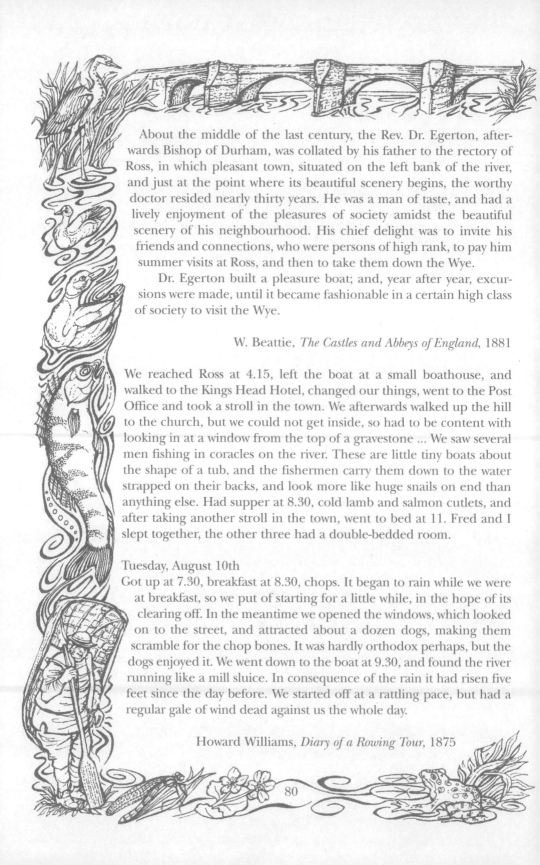

About the middle of the last century, the Rev. Dr. Egerton, afterwards Bishop of Durham, was collated by his father to the rectory of Ross, in which pleasant town, situated on the left bank of the river, and just at the point where its beautiful scenery begins, the worthy doctor resided nearly thirty years. He was a man of taste, and had a lively enjoyment of the pleasures of society amidst the beautiful scenery of his neighbourhood. His chief delight was to invite his friends and connections, who were persons of high rank, to pay him summer visits at Ross, and then to take them down the Wye.

Dr. Egerton built a pleasure boat; and, year after year, excursions were made, until it became fashionable in a certain high class of society to visit the Wye.

W. Beattie, *The Castles and Abbeys of England*, 1881

We reached Ross at 4.15, left the boat at a small boathouse, and walked to the Kings Head Hotel, changed our things, went to the Post Office and took a stroll in the town. We afterwards walked up the hill to the church, but we could not get inside, so had to be content with looking in at a window from the top of a gravestone ... We saw several men fishing in coracles on the river. These are little tiny boats about the shape of a tub, and the fishermen carry them down to the water strapped on their backs, and look more like huge snails on end than anything else. Had supper at 8.30, cold lamb and salmon cutlets, and after taking another stroll in the town, went to bed at 11. Fred and I slept together, the other three had a double-bedded room.

Tuesday, August 10th
Got up at 7.30, breakfast at 8.30, chops. It began to rain while we were at breakfast, so we put of starting for a little while, in the hope of its clearing off. In the meantime we opened the windows, which looked on to the street, and attracted about a dozen dogs, making them scramble for the chop bones. It was hardly orthodox perhaps, but the dogs enjoyed it. We went down to the boat at 9.30, and found the river running like a mill sluice. In consequence of the rain it had risen five feet since the day before. We started off at a rattling pace, but had a regular gale of wind dead against us the whole day.

Howard Williams, *Diary of a Rowing Tour*, 1875

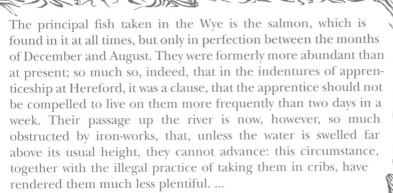

The principal fish taken in the Wye is the salmon, which is found in it at all times, but only in perfection between the months of December and August. They were formerly more abundant than at present; so much so, indeed, that in the indentures of apprenticeship at Hereford, it was a clause, that the apprentice should not be compelled to live on them more frequently than two days in a week. Their passage up the river is now, however, so much obstructed by iron-works, that, unless the water is swelled far above its usual height, they cannot advance: this circumstance, together with the illegal practice of taking them in cribs, have rendered them much less plentiful. ...

From the repute of its fish, the Wye has long been a favourite resort of the angler, who oft-times reaps a rich reward from its water for his patience and skill. Salmon of great weight and fine flavour are frequently hooked near the town.

J.A. Stratford, *The Wye Tour*, 1896

One of the most expensive items eaten by the bishop and one which attracted a high toll in Hereford market, was salmon. Salmon were as highly valued and as expensive then as they are now. The hoary old tale about apprentices' indentures having clauses stipulating that they must not be made to eat salmon more than three days a week, must have originated as a sourly ironic joke, which by endless unquestioning repetition gained the status of 'it is a well known fact'. On the contrary, it wasn't a fact and never had been.

Elizabeth Taylor, *King's Caple in Archenfield*, 1997

My first forty-pounder was killed on Guy's Hospital water with a £2 season ticket! Like many others of like weight it met its fate by aid of a glorious fluke.

I had hired a small pleasure boat from Davies (who, alas, was drowned at night a few years ago when going clotting for eels) and arranged to meet W.B.P. at the Dock at Ross. I fished the Weir End blank with a fly and then dropped downstream, to Hom Pill, which is a deep, almost streamless hole. It was a blazing hot

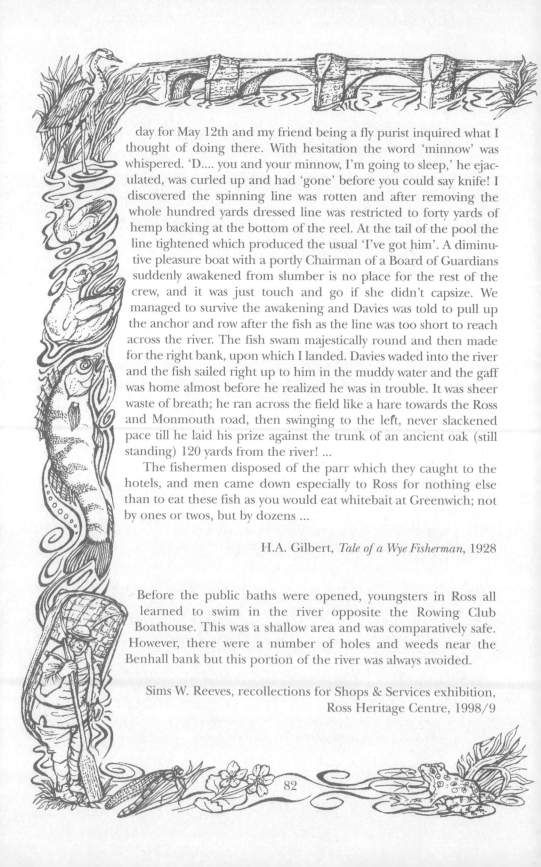

day for May 12th and my friend being a fly purist inquired what I thought of doing there. With hesitation the word 'minnow' was whispered. 'D.... you and your minnow, I'm going to sleep,' he ejaculated, was curled up and had 'gone' before you could say knife! I discovered the spinning line was rotten and after removing the whole hundred yards dressed line was restricted to forty yards of hemp backing at the bottom of the reel. At the tail of the pool the line tightened which produced the usual 'I've got him'. A diminutive pleasure boat with a portly Chairman of a Board of Guardians suddenly awakened from slumber is no place for the rest of the crew, and it was just touch and go if she didn't capsize. We managed to survive the awakening and Davies was told to pull up the anchor and row after the fish as the line was too short to reach across the river. The fish swam majestically round and then made for the right bank, upon which I landed. Davies waded into the river and the fish sailed right up to him in the muddy water and the gaff was home almost before he realized he was in trouble. It was sheer waste of breath; he ran across the field like a hare towards the Ross and Monmouth road, then swinging to the left, never slackened pace till he laid his prize against the trunk of an ancient oak (still standing) 120 yards from the river! ...

The fishermen disposed of the parr which they caught to the hotels, and men came down especially to Ross for nothing else than to eat these fish as you would eat whitebait at Greenwich; not by ones or twos, but by dozens ...

H.A. Gilbert, *Tale of a Wye Fisherman*, 1928

Before the public baths were opened, youngsters in Ross all learned to swim in the river opposite the Rowing Club Boathouse. This was a shallow area and was comparatively safe. However, there were a number of holes and weeds near the Benhall bank but this portion of the river was always avoided.

Sims W. Reeves, recollections for Shops & Services exhibition, Ross Heritage Centre, 1998/9

FOLKLORE

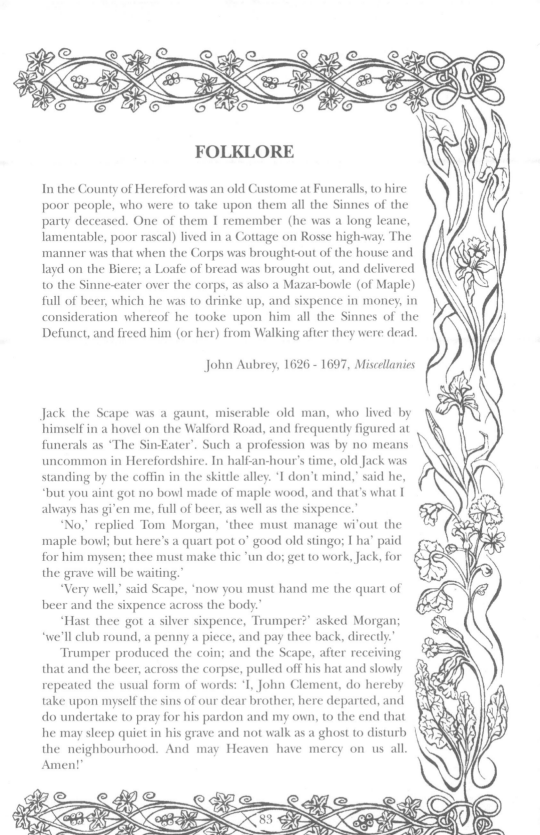

In the County of Hereford was an old Custome at Funeralls, to hire poor people, who were to take upon them all the Sinnes of the party deceased. One of them I remember (he was a long leane, lamentable, poor rascal) lived in a Cottage on Rosse high-way. The manner was that when the Corps was brought-out of the house and layd on the Biere; a Loafe of bread was brought out, and delivered to the Sinne-eater over the corps, as also a Mazar-bowle (of Maple) full of beer, which he was to drinke up, and sixpence in money, in consideration whereof he tooke upon him all the Sinnes of the Defunct, and freed him (or her) from Walking after they were dead.

John Aubrey, 1626 - 1697, *Miscellanies*

Jack the Scape was a gaunt, miserable old man, who lived by himself in a hovel on the Walford Road, and frequently figured at funerals as 'The Sin-Eater'. Such a profession was by no means uncommon in Herefordshire. In half-an-hour's time, old Jack was standing by the coffin in the skittle alley. 'I don't mind,' said he, 'but you aint got no bowl made of maple wood, and that's what I always has gi'en me, full of beer, as well as the sixpence.'

'No,' replied Tom Morgan, 'thee must manage wi'out the maple bowl; but here's a quart pot o' good old stingo; I ha' paid for him mysen; thee must make thic 'un do; get to work, Jack, for the grave will be waiting.'

'Very well,' said Scape, 'now you must hand me the quart of beer and the sixpence across the body.'

'Hast thee got a silver sixpence, Trumper?' asked Morgan; 'we'll club round, a penny a piece, and pay thee back, directly.'

Trumper produced the coin; and the Scape, after receiving that and the beer, across the corpse, pulled off his hat and slowly repeated the usual form of words: 'I, John Clement, do hereby take upon myself the sins of our dear brother, here departed, and do undertake to pray for his pardon and my own, to the end that he may sleep quiet in his grave and not walk as a ghost to disturb the neighbourhood. And may Heaven have mercy on us all. Amen!'

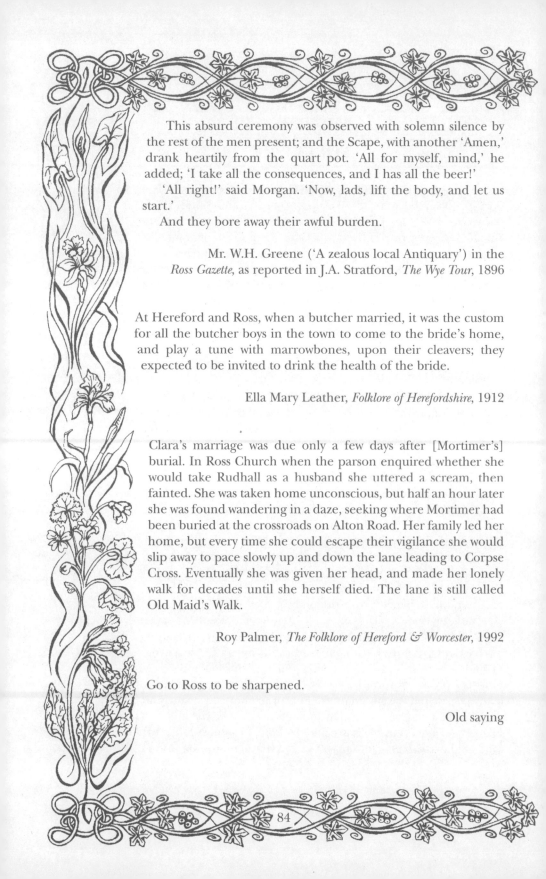

This absurd ceremony was observed with solemn silence by the rest of the men present; and the Scape, with another 'Amen,' drank heartily from the quart pot. 'All for myself, mind,' he added; 'I take all the consequences, and I has all the beer!'

'All right!' said Morgan. 'Now, lads, lift the body, and let us start.'

And they bore away their awful burden.

Mr. W.H. Greene ('A zealous local Antiquary') in the
Ross Gazette, as reported in J.A. Stratford, *The Wye Tour*, 1896

At Hereford and Ross, when a butcher married, it was the custom for all the butcher boys in the town to come to the bride's home, and play a tune with marrowbones, upon their cleavers; they expected to be invited to drink the health of the bride.

Ella Mary Leather, *Folklore of Herefordshire*, 1912

Clara's marriage was due only a few days after [Mortimer's] burial. In Ross Church when the parson enquired whether she would take Rudhall as a husband she uttered a scream, then fainted. She was taken home unconscious, but half an hour later she was found wandering in a daze, seeking where Mortimer had been buried at the crossroads on Alton Road. Her family led her home, but every time she could escape their vigilance she would slip away to pace slowly up and down the lane leading to Corpse Cross. Eventually she was given her head, and made her lonely walk for decades until she herself died. The lane is still called Old Maid's Walk.

Roy Palmer, *The Folklore of Hereford & Worcester*, 1992

Go to Ross to be sharpened.

Old saying

Corn-showing, which took place at Easter, combined a holiday and utility. Corn-showing was really weeding, pulling the corn-cockle (the Lolium of Virgil) from the field, and the one who did best was allowed to claim a kiss from the prettiest maid, and the largest piece of cake from the feast provided. Married men, I suppose, if their wives were present, took the cake and let the kiss go. The seed of corn-cockle, if it were among the wheat to be ground, therefore getting into the bread, was supposed to be poisonous, causing giddiness and vertigo. There were Harvest Homes, Maypole and Acorn dances. Ross people knew how to enjoy themselves. The young peasantry have been known to adopt the idle classical superstition of 'Love-Philtres and Powders' and there was a case recorded when a young chemist in the town, on being asked for these, indulged his sense of humour by giving an emetic instead. Cock-fighting was 'in high vogue'. Indeed, Ross would have been unique in the times if it had not been.

H.L.V Fletcher, *Portrait of the Wye Valley*, 1968

The Ross Workhouse has a small but important footnote in folk-loric history because it was here that Cecil Sharp collected some 45 songs from the inmates. Many of these are particularly good versions.

Michael Raven, *A Guide to Herefordshire*, 1996

[An] incident was remembered by an inmate of Ross workhouse ... 'He was coming over Whitney Bridge, many years ago, when behind the cart he was driving came a waggoner with three horses, and no money to pay toll. He defied the old woman at the toll house, and would have driven past her, but she witched the horses so that they would not move. "I seen it meself, them 'orses 'ouldn't muv nor stir, and when I lent the mon the toll money they went right on through. There was funny tales about that old 'ooman: folks took care they didna give her offence: 'er'd make their pigs dance in their cots till they fetched her to stop 'em."'

Roy Palmer, *The Folklore of Hereford & Worcester*, 1992

BOTANY

In a recess of the wood, east of Penyard Castle, there is still a tree called the Gospel Oak, where one formerly stood, from which the Druids explained the mysterious virtues of the mistletoe, which they so superstitiously held it to possess 'if cut with their golden pruning hooks,' &c. The old tree has been noticed from time immemorial to within this century, by that title, when referred to as one of the boundaries in the perambulations of the parish of Ross; and the present tree is therein recognized as 'the young Gospel Oak, where the old one formerly stood.' A religious ceremony is occasionally kept up on these important occasions, by reading the gospel of the day under it, which was performed in May, 1774, by the Rev. Theophilus Meredith, the Rector.

Thomas Bonner, *Ten Views of Goodrich Castle*, 1798

My attention has frequently during the last few weeks been drawn to the peculiar silky appearance of the fields of mowing grass around Ross, due to the unusual prevalence of the yellow oat-grass (*Avena flavescens*). It seems a trifling circumstance to mention, but small facts in natural history often turn out to be important ones. Like other British perennial oat-grasses, *Avena flavescens* flourishes in dry situations, and produces very few weak leafy shoots - bottom grass, as the farmer terms them. Hence these grasses are of little value for cultivation, and from their slow growth will readily be overcome by more vigorously growing kinds. The unusual plenty which I have mentioned is, I think, readily explained by the remarkable drought during the spring months of this year, which, while it retarded the growth of the more luxuriant pasture plants, supplied the precise conditions required for the healthy growth of the yellow oat, and prevented it being stifled and overrun, thus having the double effect of a stimulus and a safeguard.

W.H. Purchas, *Woolhope Transactions*, 1852-55

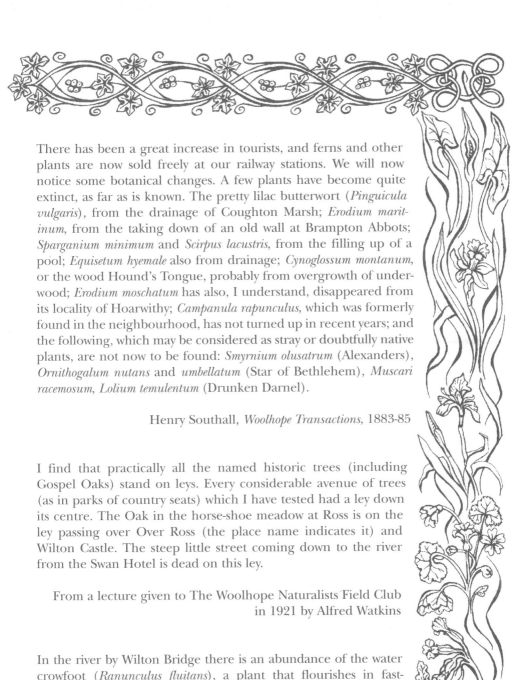

There has been a great increase in tourists, and ferns and other plants are now sold freely at our railway stations. We will now notice some botanical changes. A few plants have become quite extinct, as far as is known. The pretty lilac butterwort (*Pinguicula vulgaris*), from the drainage of Coughton Marsh; *Erodium maritinum*, from the taking down of an old wall at Brampton Abbots; *Sparganium minimum* and *Scirpus lacustris*, from the filling up of a pool; *Equisetum hyemale* also from drainage; *Cynoglossum montanum*, or the wood Hound's Tongue, probably from overgrowth of underwood; *Erodium moschatum* has also, I understand, disappeared from its locality of Hoarwithy; *Campanula rapunculus*, which was formerly found in the neighbourhood, has not turned up in recent years; and the following, which may be considered as stray or doubtfully native plants, are not now to be found: *Smyrnium olusatrum* (Alexanders), *Ornithogalum nutans* and *umbellatum* (Star of Bethlehem), *Muscari racemosum*, *Lolium temulentum* (Drunken Darnel).

Henry Southall, *Woolhope Transactions*, 1883-85

I find that practically all the named historic trees (including Gospel Oaks) stand on leys. Every considerable avenue of trees (as in parks of country seats) which I have tested had a ley down its centre. The Oak in the horse-shoe meadow at Ross is on the ley passing over Over Ross (the place name indicates it) and Wilton Castle. The steep little street coming down to the river from the Swan Hotel is dead on this ley.

From a lecture given to The Woolhope Naturalists Field Club in 1921 by Alfred Watkins

In the river by Wilton Bridge there is an abundance of the water crowfoot (*Ranunculus fluitans*), a plant that flourishes in fast-running streams, and bears a beautiful white blossom. When in full bloom here the crowfoot presents a magnificent scene, holding visitors to the old bridge in admiration sometimes for hours.

Wye Valley, Ward Lock, 1951

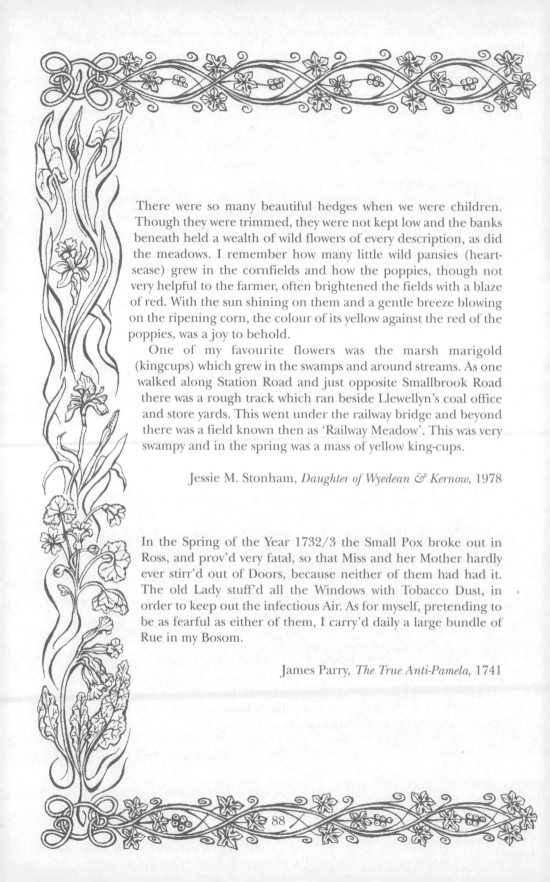

There were so many beautiful hedges when we were children. Though they were trimmed, they were not kept low and the banks beneath held a wealth of wild flowers of every description, as did the meadows. I remember how many little wild pansies (heart-sease) grew in the cornfields and how the poppies, though not very helpful to the farmer, often brightened the fields with a blaze of red. With the sun shining on them and a gentle breeze blowing on the ripening corn, the colour of its yellow against the red of the poppies, was a joy to behold.

One of my favourite flowers was the marsh marigold (kingcups) which grew in the swamps and around streams. As one walked along Station Road and just opposite Smallbrook Road there was a rough track which ran beside Llewellyn's coal office and store yards. This went under the railway bridge and beyond there was a field known then as 'Railway Meadow'. This was very swampy and in the spring was a mass of yellow king-cups.

Jessie M. Stonham, *Daughter of Wyedean & Kernow*, 1978

In the Spring of the Year 1732/3 the Small Pox broke out in Ross, and prov'd very fatal, so that Miss and her Mother hardly ever stirr'd out of Doors, because neither of them had had it. The old Lady stuff'd all the Windows with Tobacco Dust, in order to keep out the infectious Air. As for myself, pretending to be as fearful as either of them, I carry'd daily a large bundle of Rue in my Bosom.

James Parry, *The True Anti-Pamela*, 1741

DRINK

Being out at work together, Rufford had finifhed his bottle before the labour of the day was concluded, and wifhed for another draft; which Mr. Kyrle obferving, gave him his own to drink from. Rufford was a thirfty foul, and like the generality of his countrymen loved the juice of the apple; and when he got the liquor at his mouth, feemed very unwilling, from the fwig he took, to part with it, till he came to the bottom; which being what his mafter neither wifhed nor expected, he began hallooing; and when he put it down, faid, 'Ods bud, Ods bud, (his usual exclamation) Rufford, could not you hear?'

'No Sir,' fays Rufford, 'I could not hear at that time.'

Soon after Mr. Kyrle took up the bottle, and began drinking from it, when Rufford, who was at work near, ftepped before him, and began to make violent geftures with his mouth, but did not utter a word. When Mr. Kyrle laid it down, he afked Rufford, 'Why he did not halloo?' 'So I did, Sir,' replied Rufford, 'as loud as I could.'

'If you did,' fays Mr. Kyrle, 'I did not hear you.'

'Sir,' rejoins Rufford, 'did I not before tell you; That no man can hear when he is drinking.'

Charles Heath, *Excursion Down the Wye from Ross to Monmouth,*
1799

A Troop of the Right Honourable the Earl of Stair's Regiment (but now Lord Cadogan's) is quartered in Ross. Some of the young gentlemen of the surrounding country mansions resolve to hold a dancing competition for the girls of the town, but the young townsmen, knowing what the result will be, circumvent them by making the band too drunk to play. James Parry agreed to act as executor for Mrs. Hunt and as a result acquired 40 gallons of Madeira Wine in Casks, 5 Dozen in Bottles.

Anon

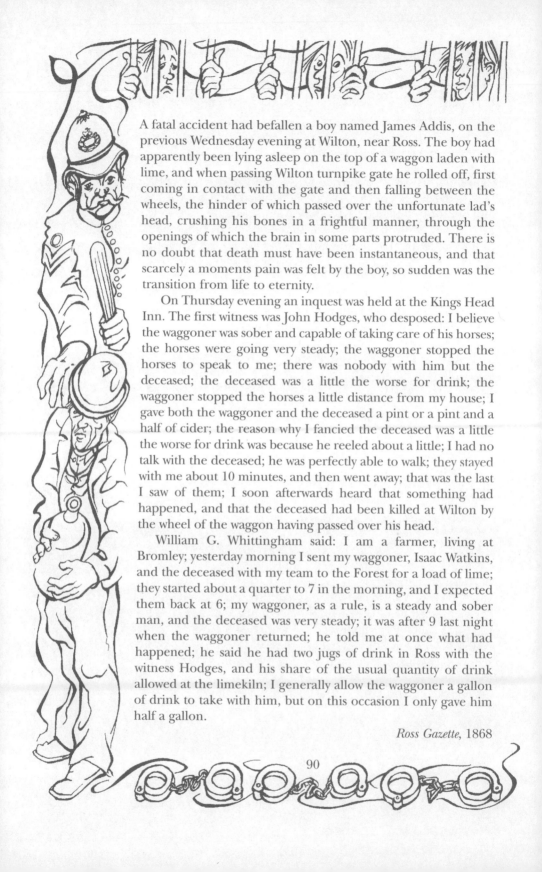

A fatal accident had befallen a boy named James Addis, on the previous Wednesday evening at Wilton, near Ross. The boy had apparently been lying asleep on the top of a waggon laden with lime, and when passing Wilton turnpike gate he rolled off, first coming in contact with the gate and then falling between the wheels, the hinder of which passed over the unfortunate lad's head, crushing his bones in a frightful manner, through the openings of which the brain in some parts protruded. There is no doubt that death must have been instantaneous, and that scarcely a moments pain was felt by the boy, so sudden was the transition from life to eternity.

On Thursday evening an inquest was held at the Kings Head Inn. The first witness was John Hodges, who desposed: I believe the waggoner was sober and capable of taking care of his horses; the horses were going very steady; the waggoner stopped the horses to speak to me; there was nobody with him but the deceased; the deceased was a little the worse for drink; the waggoner stopped the horses a little distance from my house; I gave both the waggoner and the deceased a pint or a pint and a half of cider; the reason why I fancied the deceased was a little the worse for drink was because he reeled about a little; I had no talk with the deceased; he was perfectly able to walk; they stayed with me about 10 minutes, and then went away; that was the last I saw of them; I soon afterwards heard that something had happened, and that the deceased had been killed at Wilton by the wheel of the waggon having passed over his head.

William G. Whittingham said: I am a farmer, living at Bromley; yesterday morning I sent my waggoner, Isaac Watkins, and the deceased with my team to the Forest for a load of lime; they started about a quarter to 7 in the morning, and I expected them back at 6; my waggoner, as a rule, is a steady and sober man, and the deceased was very steady; it was after 9 last night when the waggoner returned; he told me at once what had happened; he said he had two jugs of drink in Ross with the witness Hodges, and his share of the usual quantity of drink allowed at the limekiln; I generally allow the waggoner a gallon of drink to take with him, but on this occasion I only gave him half a gallon.

Ross Gazette, 1868

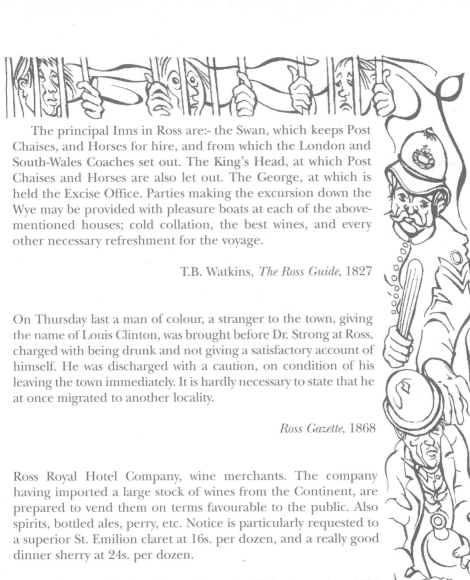

The principal Inns in Ross are:- the Swan, which keeps Post Chaises, and Horses for hire, and from which the London and South-Wales Coaches set out. The King's Head, at which Post Chaises and Horses are also let out. The George, at which is held the Excise Office. Parties making the excursion down the Wye may be provided with pleasure boats at each of the above-mentioned houses; cold collation, the best wines, and every other necessary refreshment for the voyage.

T.B. Watkins, *The Ross Guide*, 1827

On Thursday last a man of colour, a stranger to the town, giving the name of Louis Clinton, was brought before Dr. Strong at Ross, charged with being drunk and not giving a satisfactory account of himself. He was discharged with a caution, on condition of his leaving the town immediately. It is hardly necessary to state that he at once migrated to another locality.

Ross Gazette, 1868

Ross Royal Hotel Company, wine merchants. The company having imported a large stock of wines from the Continent, are prepared to vend them on terms favourable to the public. Also spirits, bottled ales, perry, etc. Notice is particularly requested to a superior St. Emilion claret at 16s. per dozen, and a really good dinner sherry at 24s. per dozen.

Advert in the *Ross Gazette*, Thursday 15th. September, 1870

These were the days of Spring and Langan in the prize-fighting ring, and imitations of these chiefs of the prize ring frequently took place in the Prospect, adjoining the old Pounds Inn and Cattle Market, where the Royal Hotel now stands. A well-known boxer named Welsh, I believe, for a wager swallowed half-a-pint of gin and killed himself.

Letter from T. Sherwood Smith, The Pynes, Keynsham,
in *The Hereford Times*, 30th January, 1889

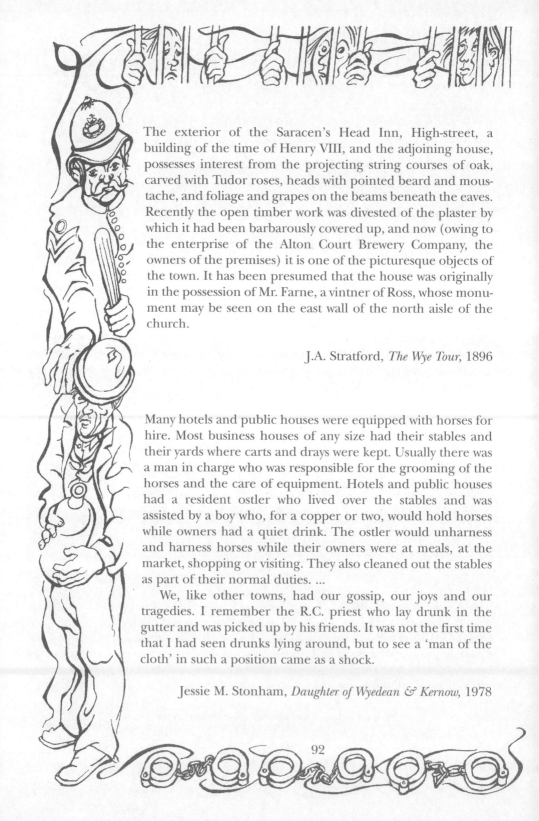

The exterior of the Saracen's Head Inn, High-street, a building of the time of Henry VIII, and the adjoining house, possesses interest from the projecting string courses of oak, carved with Tudor roses, heads with pointed beard and moustache, and foliage and grapes on the beams beneath the eaves. Recently the open timber work was divested of the plaster by which it had been barbarously covered up, and now (owing to the enterprise of the Alton Court Brewery Company, the owners of the premises) it is one of the picturesque objects of the town. It has been presumed that the house was originally in the possession of Mr. Farne, a vintner of Ross, whose monument may be seen on the east wall of the north aisle of the church.

J.A. Stratford, *The Wye Tour*, 1896

Many hotels and public houses were equipped with horses for hire. Most business houses of any size had their stables and their yards where carts and drays were kept. Usually there was a man in charge who was responsible for the grooming of the horses and the care of equipment. Hotels and public houses had a resident ostler who lived over the stables and was assisted by a boy who, for a copper or two, would hold horses while owners had a quiet drink. The ostler would unharness and harness horses while their owners were at meals, at the market, shopping or visiting. They also cleaned out the stables as part of their normal duties. ...

We, like other towns, had our gossip, our joys and our tragedies. I remember the R.C. priest who lay drunk in the gutter and was picked up by his friends. It was not the first time that I had seen drunks lying around, but to see a 'man of the cloth' in such a position came as a shock.

Jessie M. Stonham, *Daughter of Wyedean & Kernow*, 1978

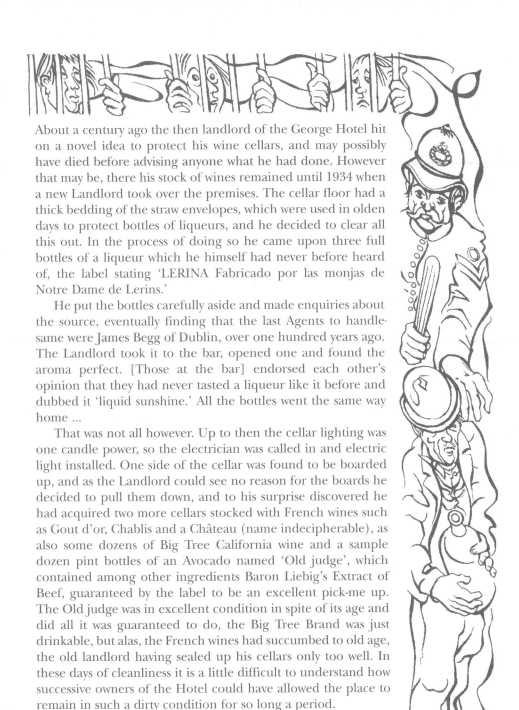

About a century ago the then landlord of the George Hotel hit on a novel idea to protect his wine cellars, and may possibly have died before advising anyone what he had done. However that may be, there his stock of wines remained until 1934 when a new Landlord took over the premises. The cellar floor had a thick bedding of the straw envelopes, which were used in olden days to protect bottles of liqueurs, and he decided to clear all this out. In the process of doing so he came upon three full bottles of a liqueur which he himself had never before heard of, the label stating 'LERINA Fabricado por las monjas de Notre Dame de Lerins.'

He put the bottles carefully aside and made enquiries about the source, eventually finding that the last Agents to handle same were James Begg of Dublin, over one hundred years ago. The Landlord took it to the bar, opened one and found the aroma perfect. [Those at the bar] endorsed each other's opinion that they had never tasted a liqueur like it before and dubbed it 'liquid sunshine.' All the bottles went the same way home ...

That was not all however. Up to then the cellar lighting was one candle power, so the electrician was called in and electric light installed. One side of the cellar was found to be boarded up, and as the Landlord could see no reason for the boards he decided to pull them down, and to his surprise discovered he had acquired two more cellars stocked with French wines such as Gout d'or, Chablis and a Château (name indecipherable), as also some dozens of Big Tree California wine and a sample dozen pint bottles of an Avocado named 'Old judge', which contained among other ingredients Baron Liebig's Extract of Beef, guaranteed by the label to be an excellent pick-me up. The Old judge was in excellent condition in spite of its age and did all it was guaranteed to do, the Big Tree Brand was just drinkable, but alas, the French wines had succumbed to old age, the old landlord having sealed up his cellars only too well. In these days of cleanliness it is a little difficult to understand how successive owners of the Hotel could have allowed the place to remain in such a dirty condition for so long a period.

Alfred Greer, *Ross, the River Wye & the Forest of Dean*, 1947

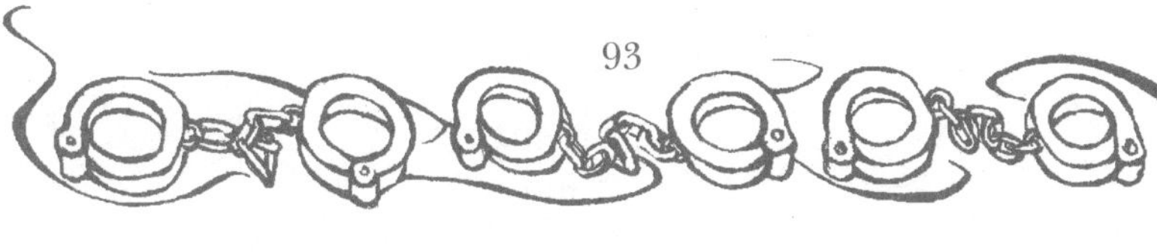

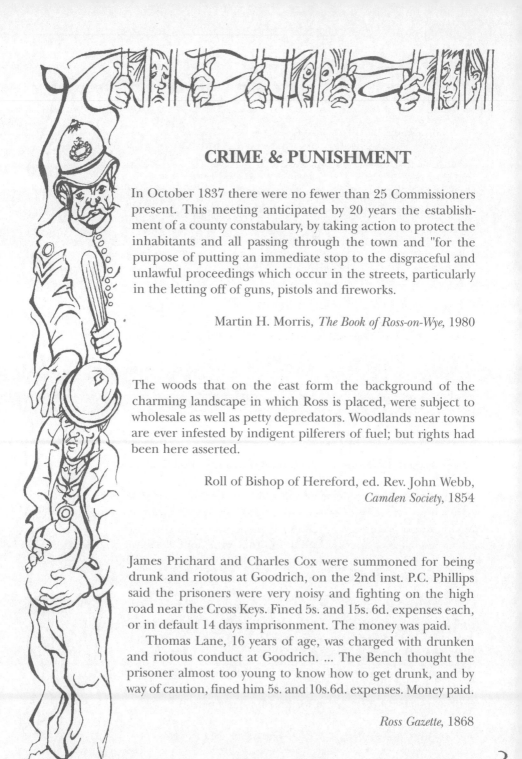

CRIME & PUNISHMENT

In October 1837 there were no fewer than 25 Commissioners present. This meeting anticipated by 20 years the establishment of a county constabulary, by taking action to protect the inhabitants and all passing through the town and "for the purpose of putting an immediate stop to the disgraceful and unlawful proceedings which occur in the streets, particularly in the letting off of guns, pistols and fireworks.

Martin H. Morris, *The Book of Ross-on-Wye*, 1980

The woods that on the east form the background of the charming landscape in which Ross is placed, were subject to wholesale as well as petty depredators. Woodlands near towns are ever infested by indigent pilferers of fuel; but rights had been here asserted.

Roll of Bishop of Hereford, ed. Rev. John Webb,
Camden Society, 1854

James Prichard and Charles Cox were summoned for being drunk and riotous at Goodrich, on the 2nd inst. P.C. Phillips said the prisoners were very noisy and fighting on the high road near the Cross Keys. Fined 5s. and 15s. 6d. expenses each, or in default 14 days imprisonment. The money was paid.

Thomas Lane, 16 years of age, was charged with drunken and riotous conduct at Goodrich. ... The Bench thought the prisoner almost too young to know how to get drunk, and by way of caution, fined him 5s. and 10s.6d. expenses. Money paid.

Ross Gazette, 1868

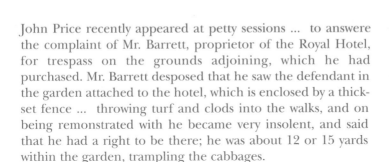

John Price recently appeared at petty sessions ... to answere the complaint of Mr. Barrett, proprietor of the Royal Hotel, for trespass on the grounds adjoining, which he had purchased. Mr. Barrett desposed that he saw the defendant in the garden attached to the hotel, which is enclosed by a thick-set fence ... throwing turf and clods into the walks, and on being remonstrated with he became very insolent, and said that he had a right to be there; he was about 12 or 15 yards within the garden, trampling the cabbages.

Hereford Journal, Wednesday 21st June, 1848

One of those accidents of so singular and strange a character that go far towards proving how suddenly an alarm or panic may be created, and yet on the other hand points in an equally strong direction towards showing the necessity for vigilance and caution on the part of the police, happened near Ross on Friday last. Between 11 and 12 o'clock in the morning of that day, a tall, thick-set young man was seen to pass along the road which leads from the Prince of Wales Inn to the Goodrich Ferry. He carried in his hand a carpet bag, which, from the peculiar way he grasped it, and the certainty impressed upon the beholder of the very limited luggage it must hold, led many people whose houses he passed, to cast more than a casual glance at him, but at the same time without any suspicion that matters were the reverse of right. Just as he had got to Lincoln Hill House, the residence of F. Beeston, Esq., and when nearly opposite the gates leading to that gentleman's house, a loud explosion was heard, and the cottagers residing in the immediate vicinity, on hastening to the spot, found that the contents of the man's carpet bag had caused the explosion. Of course the shock and alarm were great, and the rumour soon spread that the bag had contained what is now known as 'Geek' or 'Fenian Fire'. Suspicion was immediately attached to the man with the carpet bag, and hints soon were freely uttered about the probability of his being the chief of some Fenian organisation. The

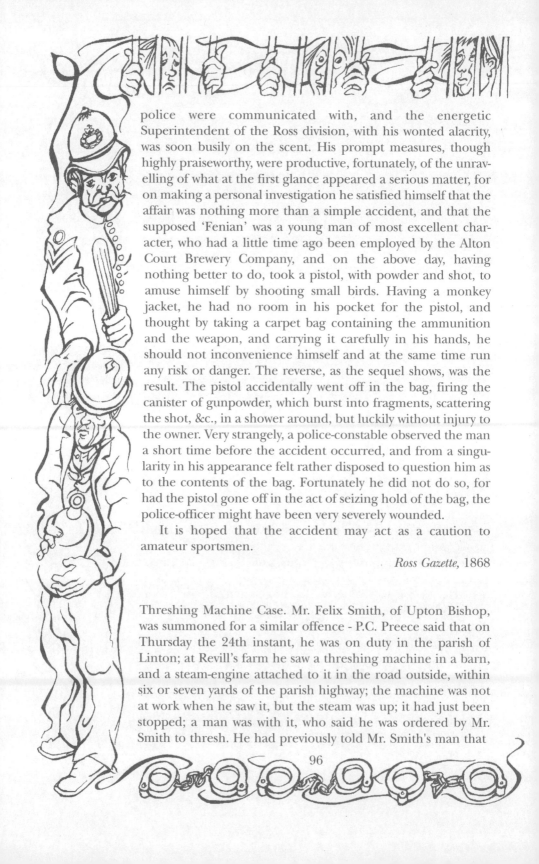

police were communicated with, and the energetic Superintendent of the Ross division, with his wonted alacrity, was soon busily on the scent. His prompt measures, though highly praiseworthy, were productive, fortunately, of the unravelling of what at the first glance appeared a serious matter, for on making a personal investigation he satisfied himself that the affair was nothing more than a simple accident, and that the supposed 'Fenian' was a young man of most excellent character, who had a little time ago been employed by the Alton Court Brewery Company, and on the above day, having nothing better to do, took a pistol, with powder and shot, to amuse himself by shooting small birds. Having a monkey jacket, he had no room in his pocket for the pistol, and thought by taking a carpet bag containing the ammunition and the weapon, and carrying it carefully in his hands, he should not inconvenience himself and at the same time run any risk or danger. The reverse, as the sequel shows, was the result. The pistol accidentally went off in the bag, firing the canister of gunpowder, which burst into fragments, scattering the shot, &c., in a shower around, but luckily without injury to the owner. Very strangely, a police-constable observed the man a short time before the accident occurred, and from a singularity in his appearance felt rather disposed to question him as to the contents of the bag. Fortunately he did not do so, for had the pistol gone off in the act of seizing hold of the bag, the police-officer might have been very severely wounded.

It is hoped that the accident may act as a caution to amateur sportsmen.

Ross Gazette, 1868

Threshing Machine Case. Mr. Felix Smith, of Upton Bishop, was summoned for a similar offence - P.C. Preece said that on Thursday the 24th instant, he was on duty in the parish of Linton; at Revill's farm he saw a threshing machine in a barn, and a steam-engine attached to it in the road outside, within six or seven yards of the parish highway; the machine was not at work when he saw it, but the steam was up; it had just been stopped; a man was with it, who said he was ordered by Mr. Smith to thresh. He had previously told Mr. Smith's man that the engine would not be allowed to work so near the road, but he had not spoken to Mr. Smith himself about it. Cross-examined by defendant; He could not say whether it was a threshing machine or a clover machine at work in the barn; it was not the first time he had seen machines of the kind at work under similar circumstances, but it was the first complaint he had made, he had made the complaint because he had recently had orders to bring these matters before the Bench. Supt. Moore said that on the day Preece saw the machine, Mr. Smith called upon him, and told him he had orders for the machine to work there, and asked him (the Supt.) to allow him to continue working there, as he had some clover which was spoiling; he told Mr. Smith that he had no power to do anything of the sort. Mr. Smith then stated that he had ordered the machine to be worked because he had some clover spoiling, and blamed the police-constable for not speaking to him on the subject.

The Magistrates, after consulting for a short time, agreed to dismiss the case.

Ross Gazette, August, 1868

Mary Williams and Emma Vaughan were charged with stealing a quantity of turnip tops, the property of William Terrett, of Huntsholme Farm. P.C. Phillips proved the case and said that he had been ordered by Mr. Terrett to take out a summons against the defendants, because persons had been continually in the habit of stealing turnip tops and taking them by the cart load to Coleford market; Mr. Terrett wished to press the charge to put a stop to the offence. The younger of the two prisoners, about 16 years old, cried bitterly during the hearing, and seemed truly contrite. The Clerk kindly remitted his fees to lighten the expenses, and the Chairman, sensibly admonishing the defendants, ordered them to pay 2s. expenses each. The poor creatures, not having a penny in their possession, were allowed a fortnight's time to pay the amount.

Ross Gazette, 1868

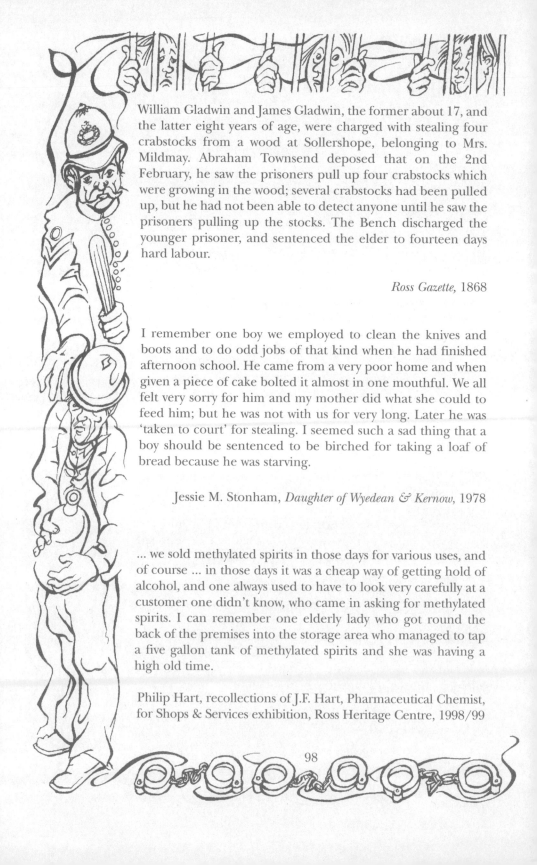

William Gladwin and James Gladwin, the former about 17, and the latter eight years of age, were charged with stealing four crabstocks from a wood at Sollershope, belonging to Mrs. Mildmay. Abraham Townsend deposed that on the 2nd February, he saw the prisoners pull up four crabstocks which were growing in the wood; several crabstocks had been pulled up, but he had not been able to detect anyone until he saw the prisoners pulling up the stocks. The Bench discharged the younger prisoner, and sentenced the elder to fourteen days hard labour.

Ross Gazette, 1868

I remember one boy we employed to clean the knives and boots and to do odd jobs of that kind when he had finished afternoon school. He came from a very poor home and when given a piece of cake bolted it almost in one mouthful. We all felt very sorry for him and my mother did what she could to feed him; but he was not with us for very long. Later he was 'taken to court' for stealing. I seemed such a sad thing that a boy should be sentenced to be birched for taking a loaf of bread because he was starving.

Jessie M. Stonham, *Daughter of Wyedean & Kernow*, 1978

... we sold methylated spirits in those days for various uses, and of course ... in those days it was a cheap way of getting hold of alcohol, and one always used to have to look very carefully at a customer one didn't know, who came in asking for methylated spirits. I can remember one elderly lady who got round the back of the premises into the storage area who managed to tap a five gallon tank of methylated spirits and she was having a high old time.

Philip Hart, recollections of J.F. Hart, Pharmaceutical Chemist, for Shops & Services exhibition, Ross Heritage Centre, 1998/99

AT WAR

Colonel Massie, governor of Gloucester, marched to Ross to prevent the junction of levies coming from Wales to join Mynne, as also to raise money for his garrison from these remoter parts. Arriving at Ross with a party of Horse and Foot, and two pieces of ordnance, he found Wilton Bridge guarded by Captain Cassie, with thirty musketeers from Goodrich Castle. By advancing a part of his Horse on the guard, he forced the river by the ford below the bridge, and getting behind the defenders compelled them, after some resistance, to leave their position. The captain was wounded and made prisoner; many of his men were killed, and the rest taken in a chase up to the castle. Massie remained some days in Ross; summoned the inhabitants to appear before him, it being his constant endeavour to add daily friends to the Parliament, and to put the country into such a posture, that upon any alarm they might gather to a head for their own defence; and many came in and declared themselves by taking the National Covenant.

The Scottish army, on its retreat from Hereford to Gloucester, repaired Wilton Bridge and entered Ross, where their ravenous rapacity, their haste and hunger, were long held in remembrance. About the same period Charles I reached Ross with an escort, on his road from Monmouth to Hereford after the surrender of Bristol; and this visit for a few hours has created a traditional report that the unfortunate king remained during a night in one of the inns.

Jakeman & Carver, *Directory & Gazetteer of Herefordshire*, 1902

[Ours] was one of the businesses which stayed open in the evenings with blackout, etc., when we had many troops who were stationed in the town at the time, particularly a lot of Americans down on the camp site where our industrial site is now, Woodville, etc. Down there it was a mass of nissen huts, and these Americans were only allowed out at night out of camp, and of course it was pitch black with no lights anywhere and they didn't know where they were or anything. Another useful little earner for small boys was taking Americans round and showing them where the pubs were! It gave them some entertainment in the evenings. Also I can remember them coming into the shop. Again we had Americans

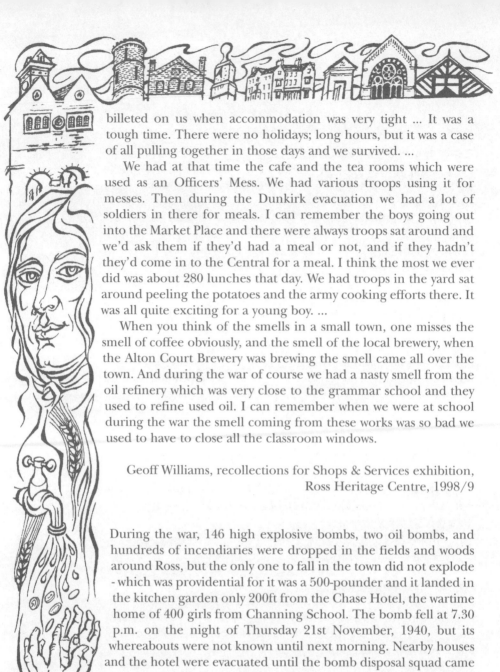

billeted on us when accommodation was very tight ... It was a tough time. There were no holidays; long hours, but it was a case of all pulling together in those days and we survived. ...

We had at that time the cafe and the tea rooms which were used as an Officers' Mess. We had various troops using it for messes. Then during the Dunkirk evacuation we had a lot of soldiers in there for meals. I can remember the boys going out into the Market Place and there were always troops sat around and we'd ask them if they'd had a meal or not, and if they hadn't they'd come in to the Central for a meal. I think the most we ever did was about 280 lunches that day. We had troops in the yard sat around peeling the potatoes and the army cooking efforts there. It was all quite exciting for a young boy. ...

When you think of the smells in a small town, one misses the smell of coffee obviously, and the smell of the local brewery, when the Alton Court Brewery was brewing the smell came all over the town. And during the war of course we had a nasty smell from the oil refinery which was very close to the grammar school and they used to refine used oil. I can remember when we were at school during the war the smell coming from these works was so bad we used to have to close all the classroom windows.

Geoff Williams, recollections for Shops & Services exhibition,
Ross Heritage Centre, 1998/9

During the war, 146 high explosive bombs, two oil bombs, and hundreds of incendiaries were dropped in the fields and woods around Ross, but the only one to fall in the town did not explode - which was providential for it was a 500-pounder and it landed in the kitchen garden only 200ft from the Chase Hotel, the wartime home of 400 girls from Channing School. The bomb fell at 7.30 p.m. on the night of Thursday 21st November, 1940, but its whereabouts were not known until next morning. Nearby houses and the hotel were evacuated until the bomb disposal squad came four days later. On another night, a plane dived over Ross, releasing a stick of bombs. The first just missed the council houses at Tudorville and the remainder fell along the river bank towards Walford.

Martin H. Morris, *The Book of Ross-on-Wye*, 1980

WILTON

Early man established a ford at Wilton where they could wade across a wide and shallow part of the Wye. An ancient road led from Whitecross in Bridstow to the bottom of Wilton Lane, it forded the Wye then followed a route, now preserved as a right of way, through a cutting in the escarpment to a place in Ross previously known as Stony Stile and on to the Dead Woman, where the Vine Tree Inn now stands. From Whitecross another road, abandoned in 1794, led directly to Wilton Castle and a possible fording beyond the fortification.

As Ross developed into a Manor of the Bishops of Hereford and a market town, a more direct route led from Wilton ford along a causeway and up a steep road now known as Wye Street. With better communications and an increase in travel and transport there became a need for the ford to be replaced by a ferry, a privilege attached to the Lord of Wilton Castle. Remains of a 14th century stone cross marks the approximate site of a ferry which conveyed men, livestock and goods across the Wye in suitable boats.

Heather Hurley, *A History of the River Crossings at Wilton-on-Wye*, 1993

In the whole extent of the Wye, through Herefordshire, there was only one bridge, that of Hereford, until the year 1597, the communication being kept open by means of boats, with Ross, Gloucester, and other places; at which time an Act of Parliament, stating in the preamble the inconveniences of the ferry, and the number of lives lost in the Passage, was then obtained for erecting a second at this place. It is a handsome structure, consisting of six arches. The arch next the village was broken down by order of General Rudhall in the wars of Charles I to impede the rebel troops in their way to Hereford.

T.B. Watkins, *The Ross Guide*, 1827

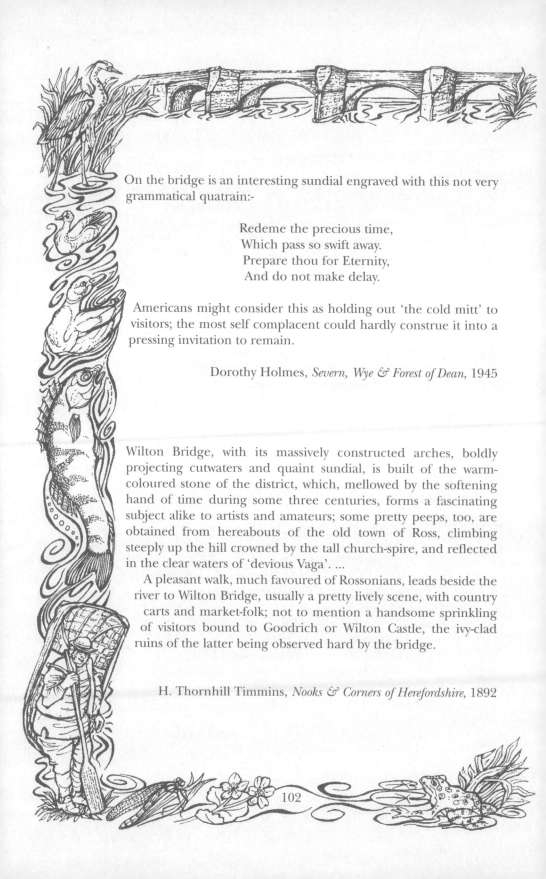

On the bridge is an interesting sundial engraved with this not very grammatical quatrain:-

> Redeme the precious time,
> Which pass so swift away.
> Prepare thou for Eternity,
> And do not make delay.

Americans might consider this as holding out 'the cold mitt' to visitors; the most self complacent could hardly construe it into a pressing invitation to remain.

Dorothy Holmes, *Severn, Wye & Forest of Dean*, 1945

Wilton Bridge, with its massively constructed arches, boldly projecting cutwaters and quaint sundial, is built of the warm-coloured stone of the district, which, mellowed by the softening hand of time during some three centuries, forms a fascinating subject alike to artists and amateurs; some pretty peeps, too, are obtained from hereabouts of the old town of Ross, climbing steeply up the hill crowned by the tall church-spire, and reflected in the clear waters of 'devious Vaga'. ...

A pleasant walk, much favoured of Rossonians, leads beside the river to Wilton Bridge, usually a pretty lively scene, with country carts and market-folk; not to mention a handsome sprinkling of visitors bound to Goodrich or Wilton Castle, the ivy-clad ruins of the latter being observed hard by the bridge.

H. Thornhill Timmins, *Nooks & Corners of Herefordshire*, 1892

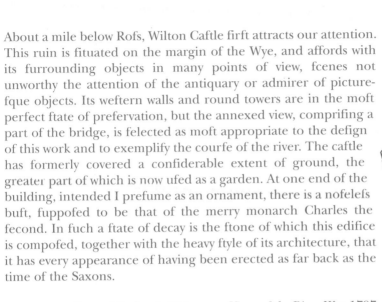

About a mile below Rofs, Wilton Caftle firft attracts our attention. This ruin is fituated on the margin of the Wye, and affords with its furrounding objects in many points of view, fcenes not unworthy the attention of the antiquary or admirer of picture-fque objects. Its weftern walls and round towers are in the moft perfect ftate of prefervation, but the annexed view, comprifing a part of the bridge, is felected as moft appropriate to the defign of this work and to exemplify the courfe of the river. The caftle has formerly covered a confiderable extent of ground, the greater part of which is now ufed as a garden. At one end of the building, intended I prefume as an ornament, there is a nofelefs buft, fuppofed to be that of the merry monarch Charles the fecond. In fuch a ftate of decay is the ftone of which this edifice is compofed, together with the heavy ftyle of its architecture, that it has every appearance of having been erected as far back as the time of the Saxons.

Samuel Ireland, *Picturesque Views of the River Wye*, 1797

As usual I was early up, after sleeping well in a large good bed, better than the looks of the inn promised, and had long break-fasted e'er Mr. O. appear'd; and whilst he was settling the bill (being appointed cashier) I walk'd down the hill and by this well built bridge, to the pretty village of Wilton, where, on the river's brink stand the ruins of Wilton Castle; in the centre of which is built a neat house, with a garden surrounded by the old bastions, and battlements; the owner suffer'd me to survey all around; and this walk and inspection of mine lasted an hour. In my return by the water side, I spoke with a patient angler, and saw one nibble.

Joseph Torrington, *Diaries*, 1787

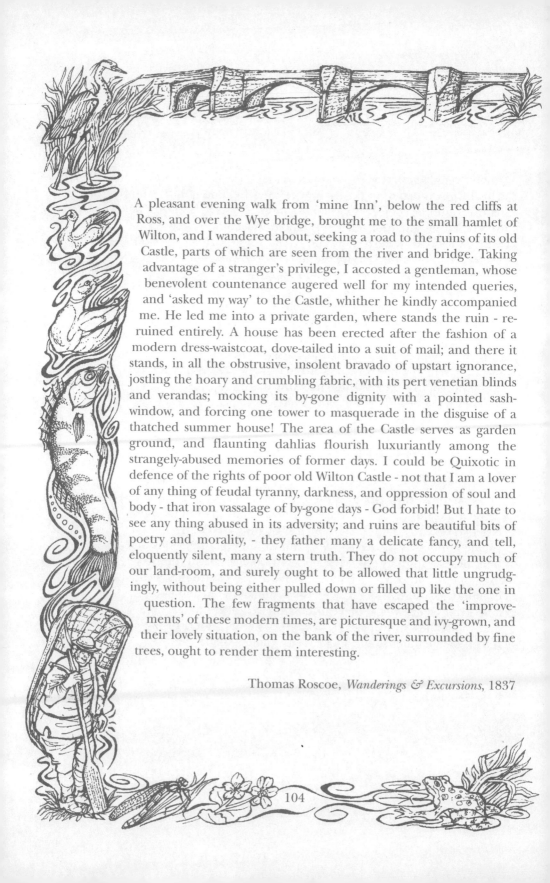

A pleasant evening walk from 'mine Inn', below the red cliffs at Ross, and over the Wye bridge, brought me to the small hamlet of Wilton, and I wandered about, seeking a road to the ruins of its old Castle, parts of which are seen from the river and bridge. Taking advantage of a stranger's privilege, I accosted a gentleman, whose benevolent countenance augered well for my intended queries, and 'asked my way' to the Castle, whither he kindly accompanied me. He led me into a private garden, where stands the ruin - re-ruined entirely. A house has been erected after the fashion of a modern dress-waistcoat, dove-tailed into a suit of mail; and there it stands, in all the obstrusive, insolent bravado of upstart ignorance, jostling the hoary and crumbling fabric, with its pert venetian blinds and verandas; mocking its by-gone dignity with a pointed sash-window, and forcing one tower to masquerade in the disguise of a thatched summer house! The area of the Castle serves as garden ground, and flaunting dahlias flourish luxuriantly among the strangely-abused memories of former days. I could be Quixotic in defence of the rights of poor old Wilton Castle - not that I am a lover of any thing of feudal tyranny, darkness, and oppression of soul and body - that iron vassalage of by-gone days - God forbid! But I hate to see any thing abused in its adversity; and ruins are beautiful bits of poetry and morality, - they father many a delicate fancy, and tell, eloquently silent, many a stern truth. They do not occupy much of our land-room, and surely ought to be allowed that little ungrudg-ingly, without being either pulled down or filled up like the one in question. The few fragments that have escaped the 'improve-ments' of these modern times, are picturesque and ivy-grown, and their lovely situation, on the bank of the river, surrounded by fine trees, ought to render them interesting.

Thomas Roscoe, *Wanderings & Excursions*, 1837

FICTION

On [an] occasion Dolby entertained his Chief at Ashfield Lodge. The late Mr. Wall, a boy at the time, remembered the visit well. he was busy setting his butterflies on the wall dividing his home from Dolby's, when Dickens approached and asked to be taken for a walk in Penyard and this was done. While Dickens was in America he made Dolby's little girl a present of a tiny pony - not much larger than a Newfoundland dog, and Miss Southall, who died less than twenty years ago, remembered how envious she felt of the little girl next door with her pony. ...

The Turkey Dolby sent to Gad's Hill did not arrive! A magnificent thirty-pounder too - the best obtainable in the neighbourhood of Ross.

On Christmas Eve came a letter:

WHERE

IS

THAT

TURKEY?

IT

HAS

NOT

ARRIVED

! ! ! ! ! !

Alas, the railway van laden with Christmas produce had caught fire on the way and only charred bits remained!

A week or two later Dickens paid his last visit to Ross. The Dolbys were now at Wilton House and the author spent a weekend there. On the Sunday afternoon the two friends, both keen pedestrians, set out to walk to Monmouth (but not back). On the way they met some youths and one of those recognized Dickens - much to his gratification.

Winifred Leeds, unpublished Mss, Hereford Record Office

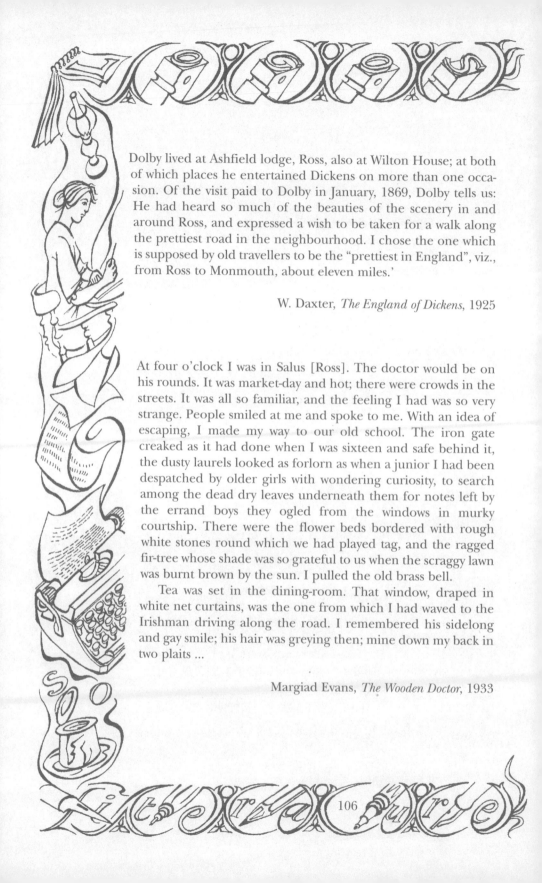

Dolby lived at Ashfield lodge, Ross, also at Wilton House; at both of which places he entertained Dickens on more than one occasion. Of the visit paid to Dolby in January, 1869, Dolby tells us: He had heard so much of the beauties of the scenery in and around Ross, and expressed a wish to be taken for a walk along the prettiest road in the neighbourhood. I chose the one which is supposed by old travellers to be the "prettiest in England", viz., from Ross to Monmouth, about eleven miles.'

W. Daxter, *The England of Dickens*, 1925

At four o'clock I was in Salus [Ross]. The doctor would be on his rounds. It was market-day and hot; there were crowds in the streets. It was all so familiar, and the feeling I had was so very strange. People smiled at me and spoke to me. With an idea of escaping, I made my way to our old school. The iron gate creaked as it had done when I was sixteen and safe behind it, the dusty laurels looked as forlorn as when a junior I had been despatched by older girls with wondering curiosity, to search among the dead dry leaves underneath them for notes left by the errand boys they ogled from the windows in murky courtship. There were the flower beds bordered with rough white stones round which we had played tag, and the ragged fir-tree whose shade was so grateful to us when the scraggy lawn was burnt brown by the sun. I pulled the old brass bell.

Tea was set in the dining-room. That window, draped in white net curtains, was the one from which I had waved to the Irishman driving along the road. I remembered his sidelong and gay smile; his hair was greying then; mine down my back in two plaits ...

Margiad Evans, *The Wooden Doctor*, 1933

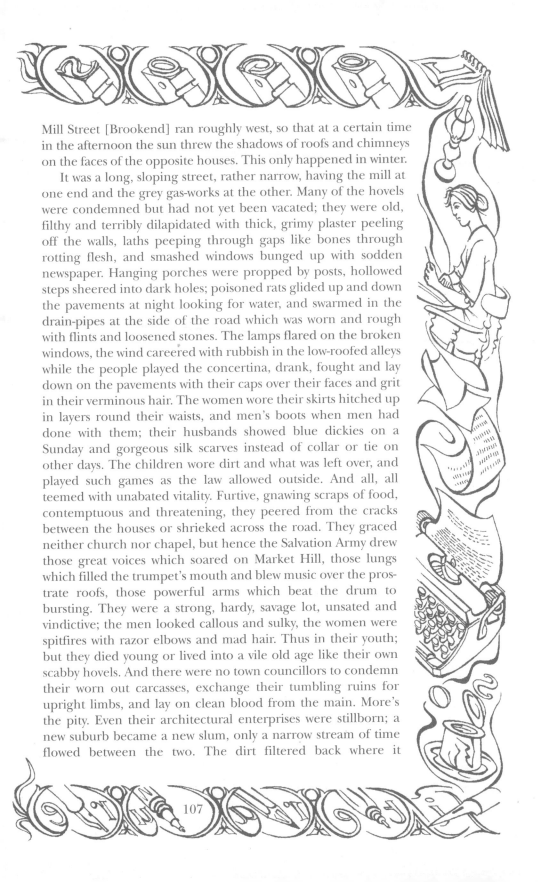

Mill Street [Brookend] ran roughly west, so that at a certain time in the afternoon the sun threw the shadows of roofs and chimneys on the faces of the opposite houses. This only happened in winter.

It was a long, sloping street, rather narrow, having the mill at one end and the grey gas-works at the other. Many of the hovels were condemned but had not yet been vacated; they were old, filthy and terribly dilapidated with thick, grimy plaster peeling off the walls, laths peeping through gaps like bones through rotting flesh, and smashed windows bunged up with sodden newspaper. Hanging porches were propped by posts, hollowed steps sheered into dark holes; poisoned rats glided up and down the pavements at night looking for water, and swarmed in the drain-pipes at the side of the road which was worn and rough with flints and loosened stones. The lamps flared on the broken windows, the wind careered with rubbish in the low-roofed alleys while the people played the concertina, drank, fought and lay down on the pavements with their caps over their faces and grit in their verminous hair. The women wore their skirts hitched up in layers round their waists, and men's boots when men had done with them; their husbands showed blue dickies on a Sunday and gorgeous silk scarves instead of collar or tie on other days. The children wore dirt and what was left over, and played such games as the law allowed outside. And all, all teemed with unabated vitality. Furtive, gnawing scraps of food, contemptuous and threatening, they peered from the cracks between the houses or shrieked across the road. They graced neither church nor chapel, but hence the Salvation Army drew those great voices which soared on Market Hill, those lungs which filled the trumpet's mouth and blew music over the prostrate roofs, those powerful arms which beat the drum to bursting. They were a strong, hardy, savage lot, unsated and vindictive; the men looked callous and sulky, the women were spitfires with razor elbows and mad hair. Thus in their youth; but they died young or lived into a vile old age like their own scabby hovels. And there were no town councillors to condemn their worn out carcasses, exchange their tumbling ruins for upright limbs, and lay on clean blood from the main. More's the pity. Even their architectural enterprises were stillborn; a new suburb became a new slum, only a narrow stream of time flowed between the two. The dirt filtered back where it

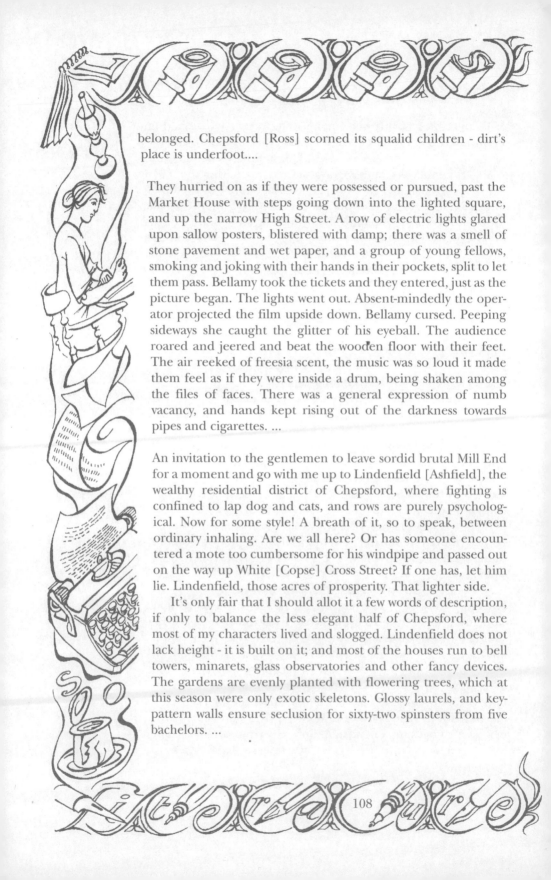

belonged. Chepsford [Ross] scorned its squalid children - dirt's place is underfoot....

They hurried on as if they were possessed or pursued, past the Market House with steps going down into the lighted square, and up the narrow High Street. A row of electric lights glared upon sallow posters, blistered with damp; there was a smell of stone pavement and wet paper, and a group of young fellows, smoking and joking with their hands in their pockets, split to let them pass. Bellamy took the tickets and they entered, just as the picture began. The lights went out. Absent-mindedly the operator projected the film upside down. Bellamy cursed. Peeping sideways she caught the glitter of his eyeball. The audience roared and jeered and beat the wooden floor with their feet. The air reeked of freesia scent, the music was so loud it made them feel as if they were inside a drum, being shaken among the files of faces. There was a general expression of numb vacancy, and hands kept rising out of the darkness towards pipes and cigarettes. ...

An invitation to the gentlemen to leave sordid brutal Mill End for a moment and go with me up to Lindenfield [Ashfield], the wealthy residential district of Chepsford, where fighting is confined to lap dog and cats, and rows are purely psychological. Now for some style! A breath of it, so to speak, between ordinary inhaling. Are we all here? Or has someone encountered a mote too cumbersome for his windpipe and passed out on the way up White [Copse] Cross Street? If one has, let him lie. Lindenfield, those acres of prosperity. That lighter side.

It's only fair that I should allot it a few words of description, if only to balance the less elegant half of Chepsford, where most of my characters lived and slogged. Lindenfield does not lack height - it is built on it; and most of the houses run to bell towers, minarets, glass observatories and other fancy devices. The gardens are evenly planted with flowering trees, which at this season were only exotic skeletons. Glossy laurels, and key-pattern walls ensure seclusion for sixty-two spinsters from five bachelors. ...

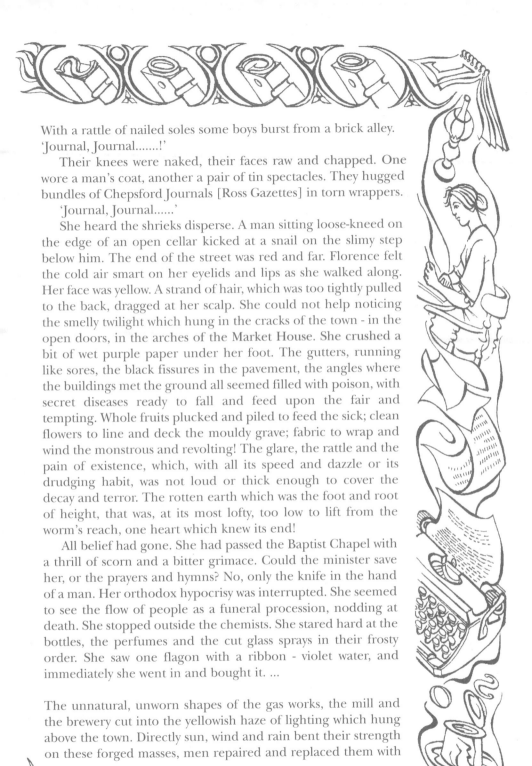

With a rattle of nailed soles some boys burst from a brick alley. 'Journal, Journal.......!'

Their knees were naked, their faces raw and chapped. One wore a man's coat, another a pair of tin spectacles. They hugged bundles of Chepsford Journals [Ross Gazettes] in torn wrappers.

'Journal, Journal......'

She heard the shrieks disperse. A man sitting loose-kneed on the edge of an open cellar kicked at a snail on the slimy step below him. The end of the street was red and far. Florence felt the cold air smart on her eyelids and lips as she walked along. Her face was yellow. A strand of hair, which was too tightly pulled to the back, dragged at her scalp. She could not help noticing the smelly twilight which hung in the cracks of the town - in the open doors, in the arches of the Market House. She crushed a bit of wet purple paper under her foot. The gutters, running like sores, the black fissures in the pavement, the angles where the buildings met the ground all seemed filled with poison, with secret diseases ready to fall and feed upon the fair and tempting. Whole fruits plucked and piled to feed the sick; clean flowers to line and deck the mouldy grave; fabric to wrap and wind the monstrous and revolting! The glare, the rattle and the pain of existence, which, with all its speed and dazzle or its drudging habit, was not loud or thick enough to cover the decay and terror. The rotten earth which was the foot and root of height, that was, at its most lofty, too low to lift from the worm's reach, one heart which knew its end!

All belief had gone. She had passed the Baptist Chapel with a thrill of scorn and a bitter grimace. Could the minister save her, or the prayers and hymns? No, only the knife in the hand of a man. Her orthodox hypocrisy was interrupted. She seemed to see the flow of people as a funeral procession, nodding at death. She stopped outside the chemists. She stared hard at the bottles, the perfumes and the cut glass sprays in their frosty order. She saw one flagon with a ribbon - violet water, and immediately she went in and bought it. ...

The unnatural, unworn shapes of the gas works, the mill and the brewery cut into the yellowish haze of lighting which hung above the town. Directly sun, wind and rain bent their strength on these forged masses, men repaired and replaced them with

sharp new outlines. They belonged to nothing but ingenuity,
strange and disturbing idols which served human purposes as
gods must serve. A steeple was now different; it might have been
erected by the spirit. Yet the mill chimney pointed the same path
and seemed grimed by efforts to attain it. Dollbright pursued
his frequent invisible tracks along Mill Street. Here, with poor
and patient living, is the frenzy which often kindles it to blazing
catastrophe and death. Down those steps a maddened lorry
driver flung his wife, breaking both her legs; from this door a
brawl started which finished half a mile away with one man
hammering another's skull upon the pavement; over this
squalid pub, reeking, ill-lit, two brothers fought, and one died,
for its possession. ...

Ha, what a town! What a vital, wicked boisterous town, which
beneath its vigorous life, conceals a black current of despair
and misery, and what people! Wild, vehement, laughing, whose
two hands are generosity and vice, and whose eyes are weapons!
There are none like them in all the rest of England, unbeliev-
able as they are to these civil gentlemen in collars and - never
mind. I speak the truth, but the gentlemen will not be
convinced. It is enough if they can be left to see this secret and
defended country, with its red fields, flogged by the rain, its
floods, storms in the elms, clouds tossed over the hills and
dissolving in moonlight, wild moods in unleashed winds and
pathetic stillnesses. If they can feel its power of height and
valley. I am possessed with it. I see it night and day. Well, that's
nothing. I am young and the gentlemen say that when I am
older I shall learn better. I shall then write of a country and its
quaint customs preening themselves in old-world nooks. That
will please them, and I shall be enriched by their pedantic pleasure to such a degree of tin-wheeled liberty that the world itself
will be no more to me than an unloved province, and belief
shrink to the length of my sight - which is short.

    The street was narrow, like a canon cleft in sulphur-coloured
brick; it was sickly with the smell of boiling from the brewery.
Rows of gloomy incavated windows stared straight into their
opposites. A yellow lorry leaning in the gutter cast a reflection
on the wet asphalt.

Margiad Evans, *Creed*, 1936

BIBLIOGRAPHY

Andere, Mary *Homes & Houses of Herefordshire*, 1977

Anglo-Saxon Chronicles, 9th-12th century, Trans. and collated by Anne Savage, Tiger Books

Aubrey, John *Miscellanies*

Bannister, Rev. T.A. *The Place Names of Herefordshire*, CUP, 1916

Beattie, W. *The Castles & Abbeys of England*, 1881

Bevan G.P. *The Wye & Its Neighbourhood*, Edward Stanford, 1887

Bloomfield, Robert *The Banks of the Wye*, Longman, Hurst, Rees, Orme, Brown and Arthur, 1813

Blount, Thomas *Manuscript History of Herefordshire*, c.1675, transcribed and researched by Richard and Catherine Botzum

Bonner, Thomas *Ten Views of Goodrich Castle*, 1798

Bradley A.C. *The Wye*, A & C Black, 1916

Burrow, Edward J. *Wye Valley Illustrated Guide Hereford to Chepstow*, 4th Edn., No.6, 1905

Camden *Britannia*, 1584

Cash, J. Allen *The River Wye*, Chapman & Hall, 1952

Cassey, Edward *History, Topography & Directory of Herefordshire*, 1858

Cobbett, William *Rural Rides* 1830, Vol.I, 1853 (Penguin Books, 1967)

Cooke, William Henry *Collections Towards the History & Antiquities of the County of Hereford*, John Murray, 1882

Daniels, Stephen & Charles Watkins *The Picturesque Landscape, Vision of Georgian Herefordshire*, University of Nottingham Department of Geology, 1994

Daxter, W. *The England of Dickens*, Cecil Palmer, 1925

Defoe, Daniel *A Tour through the Whole Island of Great Britain* ed. Rogers, Pat, Webb & Bower, 1989

Evans, Margiad (Peggy Whistler) *The Wooden Doctor*, Basil Blackwell, 1933 *Creed*, Basil Blackwell, 1936

Farrington, Joseph *Diaries*, Vol.II, August 28th - Sept. 13th, 1803, ed. James Greig, Hutchinson & Co., 1804

Fletcher, H.L.V. *Portrait of the Wye Valley*, Robert Hale, 1968

Foord, Edward *Cathedrals, Abbeys & Famous Churches*, 1925

Fosbroke, Rev. T.D. *Wye Tour*, various dates

Gilbert, H.A. *The Tale of a Wye Fisherman*, Jonathan Cape, 1928

Gilpin, William *Observations of the River Wye*, 1793

Glover, Mark and Celia *The Ross & Monmouth Railway*, Brewin Books, 1983 & 1994

Greer, Alfred *Ross, the River Wye & the Forest of Dean from Roman Times to the Present Day*, 1947

Hart, Philip recollections of J.F. Hart, Pharmaceutical Chemist, taped by the
    Ross Oral History Group of U3A for Shops & Services exhibition at Ross
    Heritage Centre, 1998/9
Heath, Charles *The Excursion Down the Wye from Ross to Monmouth*, various dates
Hearne, Thomas *Remarks & Collections* eds. C.E. Doble & D.W. Rannie
Hereford Anthology of Prose and Verse complied and edited by S.F. Gavin
    Robinson, Reprodux, 1984
Holmes, Dorothy *Severn, Wye and Forest of Dean*, Wildings & Son, 1945
Hurley, Heather *The Old Roads of South Herefordshire*, Pound House, 1992
    A History of the River Crossings at Wilton-on-Wye, Ross-on-Wye and District
        Civic Society Pink Publications No.3, 1993
Hurley, Jon *Thomas Blake, the Pious Benefactor*, Ross-on-Wye and District
    Civic Society Pink Publications No.8, 1996
Hutton, Edward *A Book of The Wye*, Methuen, 1911
Ireland, Samuel *Picturesque Views of the River Wye*, 1797
Jakeman & Carver *Directory & Gazetteer of Herefordshire*, 1902
James, James Henry *Herefordia*, 1861
Kissack, Keith *The River Wye*, Timothy Dalton, 1978
Leather, Ella Mary *Folklore of Herefordshire*, Jakeman & Carver, 1912
Leeds, Winifred Unpublished Mss, 1891, Hereford Record Office
Leland, John *Itinerary, Travels in Tudor England 1530-40*, modern edition ed.
    John Chandler, Alan Sutton, 1993
Lewis, Samuel *A Topographical Dictionary of England*, 5th edn., Vol 3 (of 4), 1845
Lewis, Rev. T.T., 1854
Littlebury's *Postal and Commercial Directory and Gazetteer of the County of
    Herefordshire*, 1867
Mais, S. *Highways & Byways in the Welsh Marches*, 1939
Mee, Arthur *The King's England*, 1948
Morgan, C.A. Virginia and Joyce M. Briffet *The Ross Workhouse, 1836-1914*,
    Ross-on-Wye and District Civic Society
Morris, Martin H. *The Book of Ross-on-Wye*, Barracuda, 1980
Morton, H.V. *In Search of England*, Methuen, 1927
Nicholls, George *Seventy Four Years in Hardware*, taped by the Ross Oral History
    Group of U3A for Shops & Services exhibition at Ross Heritage Centre,
    1998/9
Palmer, Roy *The Folklore of Hereford & Worcester*, Logaston Press, 1992
Parry J. *The True Anti-Pamela, or Memoirs of James Parry, late organist of Ross in
    Herefordshire*, 1741
Paterson's Roads, 18th edn., Longman, Rees, Orme, Brown and Green, 1826
Phillips, John *Cider*, 1791
Purchas, H. *Woolhope Transactions*, 1852-55
Raven, Michael *A Guide to Herefordshire*, 1996
Read, Rev. C. *Memorials of Old Herefordshire*, Bemrose & Sons, 1904
Reeves, Sims W. *The Kyrle Picture Palace*, taped by the Ross Oral History Group
    of U3A for Shops & Services exhibition at Ross Heritage Centre, 1998/9
Riley, Kate E. *Marie Suron, Tales of Old Ross*, The Ross Gazette, 1921

Ritchie, Leith *Narrative of a Pedestrian Ramble*, 1839

Roscoe, Thomas *Wanderings & Excursions in South Wales, Including the River Wye*, 1837

Sale, Richard *The Wye Valley*, Wildwood House, 1984

Sant, Jonathan *The Healing Wells of Herefordshire*, Moondial, 1994

Smart, Rev. W.J. *Where the Wye & Severn Flow*, 1949

Southall, H, *Woolhope Transactions*, 1883-5

Stonham, Jessie M. *Daughter of Wyedean & Kernow*, Thornhill Press, 1978

Stratford, J.A. *The Wye Tour, History of Ross*, 1896

Strong, G. *Handbook to Ross & Archenfield*, Powle, 1863

Taylor, Elizabeth *King's Caple in Archenfield*, Logaston Press, 1997

Thorn, Frank & Caroline (eds.) *Domesday Book*, Phillimore, 1983

Timmins, H. Thorneyhill *Nooks & Corners of Herefordshire*, Elliot Stock, 1892

Torrington, Hon. John Byng, 5th Viscount Torrington *Diaries*, 1934

Ward Lock *Wye Valley, Hereford & Worcester Red Guide* eds. Hammond, Reginald J.W. and Kenneth E. Lowther, 1951

Watkins, J.B. *Wye Tour*, 1896

Watkins, T.B. *The Ross Guide*, 1827

Webb, Rev. John (ed.) *A Roll of the Household Expenses of Richard de Swinfield, Bishop of Hereford*, Camden Society, 1854

West, John and Margaret *A History of Herefordshire*, Phillimore, 1985

Williams, Geoff *Central Bakery and Café*, taped by the Ross Oral History Group of U3A for Shops & Services exhibition at Ross Heritage Centre, 1998/9

Williams, Howard *Diary of a Rowing Tour*, 1875 & Alan Sutton, 1982

Woods, K.S. *Development of Country Towns in the S.W. Midlands During the 1960s*, 1968

Also:

Hereford Journal 1795, 1838, 1848

Hereford Times 1889

Ross Gazette 1868, 1869, 1870, 1879, 1890, 1891

Also from Logaston Press

The Herefordshire School of Romanesque Sculpture
by Malcolm Thurlby
192pp with 240 photographs   ISBN 1 873827 60 1   £12.95

This highly illustrated book serves as both a Guide to the surviving work of the Herefordshire School, and provides a history of the school itself. It compares the work, both in stone and other materials, in Herefordshire, Gloucestershire, Worcestershire and beyond, with that of other styles both at home and abroad— Celtic motifs, Romano-British and Anglo-Saxon work, as well as sculpture in France and Spain. The book also considers the sources of inspiration and who the patrons were and their motives. It looks at the training of the sculptors and their role in the building work, and considers whose hands may have been at work on which sites.

An Endless Quiet Valley. John Masefield, a re-evaluation
by Paul Binding
240pp with 24 illustrations
Hbk ISBN 1 873827 35 0   £17.95   Pbk ISBN 1 873827 30 X   £9.95

A literary re-appraisal of John Masefield by Paul Binding, previously deputy literary editor of the *New Statesman*. Paul considers that Masefield's period that commenced with 'The Everlasting Mercy' and continued with several narrative poems, sonnets and other work into the 1920s, to be his canon—a canon that shocked then, and can shock now. Paul sets Masefield's work in the context of other literary work that was appearing and the attitudes of the time, considers the man himself, and the passions and complexity which made him write as he did.

The Folklore of (old) Monmouthshire
by Roy Palmer
304pp with 150 illustrations   ISBN 1 873827 40 7   £12.95
This book surveys the folklore and customs of 'old' Monmouthshire, the county as it was until 1974, an area now covered by the councils of Newport, Torfaen, Blaenau Gwent, Caerphilly (in the case of Islwyn and the Rhymney Valley) and the 'new' Monmouthshire. The subject is broken down into themes: saints, the supernatural, industrial and agricultural traditions, historical beliefs and traditions, calendar customs, the beliefs and practices surrounding everyday life and death. The sources are numerous, for Roy Palmer has a wealth of folkloric knowledge built up over years of research into the subject. Includes a comprehensive index.